Better Homes and Gardens.

CHRISTMAS CRAFTS

TO MAKE AHEAD

© 1983 by Meredith Corporation, Des Moines, Iowa.
All Rights Reserved. Printed in the United States of America.
First Edition. First Printing.
Library of Congress Catalog Card Number: 82-80526
ISBN: 0-696-00885-8

BETTER HOMES AND GARDENS® BOOKS

Editor: Gerald M. Knox
Art Director: Ernest Shelton
Managing Editor: David A. Kirchner

Crafts Editor: Nancy Lindemeyer
Senior Crafts Books Editor: Joan Cravens
Associate Crafts Books Editors: Debra Felton,
    Laura Holtorf, James A. Williams

Associate Art Director (Managing): Randall Yontz
Associate Art Directors (Creative): Linda Ford,
    Neoma Alt West
Copy and Production Editors: Marsha Jahns, Nancy
    Nowiszewski, Mary Helen Schiltz, David A. Walsh
Assistant Art Director (Managing): Harijs Priekulis
Assistant Art Director (Creative): Tom Wegner
Graphic Designers: Mike Burns, Alisann Dixon,
    Mike Eagleton, Lynda Haupert, Deb Miner,
    Lyne Neymeyer, Stan Sams, D. Greg Thompson,
    Darla Whipple, Paul Zimmerman

Editor in Chief: Neil Kuehnl
Group Editorial Services Director: Duane Gregg

General Manager: Fred Stines
Director of Publishing: Robert B. Nelson
Director of Retail Marketing: Jamie Martin
Director of Direct Marketing: Arthur Heydendael

Christmas Crafts to Make Ahead

Crafts Editor: Debra Felton
Copy and Production Editor: Nancy Nowiszewski
Graphic Designer: D. Greg Thompson

Contents

EACH & EVERY TRIM A TREASURE

From us to you—here is a fabulous collection of trims and accessories to craft for Christmas! We've begun our book with heirloom ornaments for your family tree. Many of the designs, like these florals, adapt easily to other decorations, such as the garland tree skirt pictured here. All offer hours of crafting pleasure. And what a wonderful way to spread the holiday spirit all through the year! Directions begin on page 6.

By changing the pattern size and using different craft techniques, you can adapt this graceful floral garland to ornaments, a tree skirt, and stockings as shown on pages 4-5.

Ornaments

MATERIALS

2½- and 3-inch-diameter glass ornaments with mirror-finish silver on the outside
⅛-, ¼-, and ½-inch-diameter wooden dowels
Plastic foam blocks
⅝-inch-wide lettering brush
Gesso, distilled water
No. 000 and No. 8 sable brushes
Oil paints in naphthol crimson, yellow medium azo, and hooker's green
High-gloss urethane varnish
Glossy off-white enamel
Tissue paper, graphite paper
Rubbing alcohol, paint thinner

INSTRUCTIONS

For racks on which to paint and dry ornaments, cut dowels into 9-inch lengths; push them into blocks. Use ½-inch dowels for 3-inch ornaments, ¼-inch dowels for 2½-inch ornaments.

Remove the ornament caps; set aside. Clean the ornaments with a rag and rubbing alcohol; let dry.

Mix equal parts of gesso and distilled water; apply to ornaments using a ⅝-inch brush. Brush solution around the ornament stem; cover the ornament with vertical strokes. Let ornaments dry for three hours.

Trace the full-size patterns, *opposite*, onto a sheet of tissue paper. With the graphite paper, *lightly* transfer the patterns to ornaments. Paint flowers with a large brush and vines with a small brush. Varnish when dry.

Dip the metal caps in white enamel; string on a ⅛-inch dowel. Let dry for 24 hours.

Tree Skirt

MATERIALS

2¼ yards (45-inch-wide) muslin
¼ yard each of green, dark red, and light red cotton prints
Scraps of yellow fabric
Narrow and wide green double-fold bias tape
1¼ yards quilt batting or fleece

INSTRUCTIONS

On half of the muslin fabric, draw a 36-inch-diameter circle. Enlarge the floral design on the stocking, *right*, adding ¼-inch seam margins; cut six each dark and light red flowers, 40 leaves, and 12 yellow circles.

Arrange appliqués on muslin, spacing dark red flowers evenly around the circle with centers about 3½ inches from raw edge. Place light red flowers in between dark ones, with centers about 9 inches from raw edge.

Referring to the photograph, join flowers with graceful stems made from narrow bias tape. (Do not unfold tape.) Cut tape long enough to connect flowers, plus ¼ inch on each end to tuck under the flowers. Place a yellow circle in center of each flower. Arrange the leaves next to stems. Baste pieces in place.

Draw and cut a line from the center of the circle to edge. Cut two 1¼x19-inch strips of muslin. Partially bind raw edges of slit by sewing strips to right side, using a ¼-inch seam. Fold and press to the inside; do not stitch until quilting is complete.

Whipstitch all appliqués in place, turning under the raw edges as you stitch.

From remaining muslin, cut backing to match top. Sandwich fleece or batting between top and backing. Baste and quilt.

Cut a hole, 5 inches in diameter, in the center of the skirt. Finish binding the slit with the muslin. Cut out the skirt, adding ½-inch seam margins. Bind edges with wide bias tape.

Stocking

MATERIALS

½ yard of muslin
Scraps of green, dark red, and light red prints; yellow fabric
Green wide bias tape
Fleece or quilt batting
6½ inches green narrow double-fold bias tape for stem

INSTRUCTIONS

Enlarge pattern, *below*. Trace onto muslin, adding a ½-inch seam allowance around stocking. Adding ¼-inch seam allowances, cut 1 dark red flower, 6 leaves, and 1 yellow circle.

Whipstitch pieces in place on the stocking front. Cut out the stocking; cut muslin backing to match front. Sandwich fleece between the front and backing; quilt around appliqués.

From muslin, cut a stocking back the same size as front. Using bias tape, bind raw edges of the tops of front and back. Fold tops to outside as indicated on the pattern; baste. With wrong sides facing, sew stocking front to back. Bind raw edges with wide bias tape.

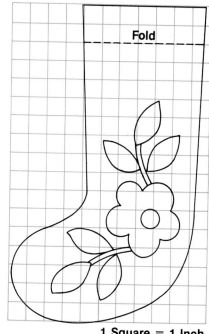

Fold

1 Square = 1 Inch

PAINTED FLORAL ORNAMENTS

Stems & leaves-Green
Flowers-Red
Centers-Yellow

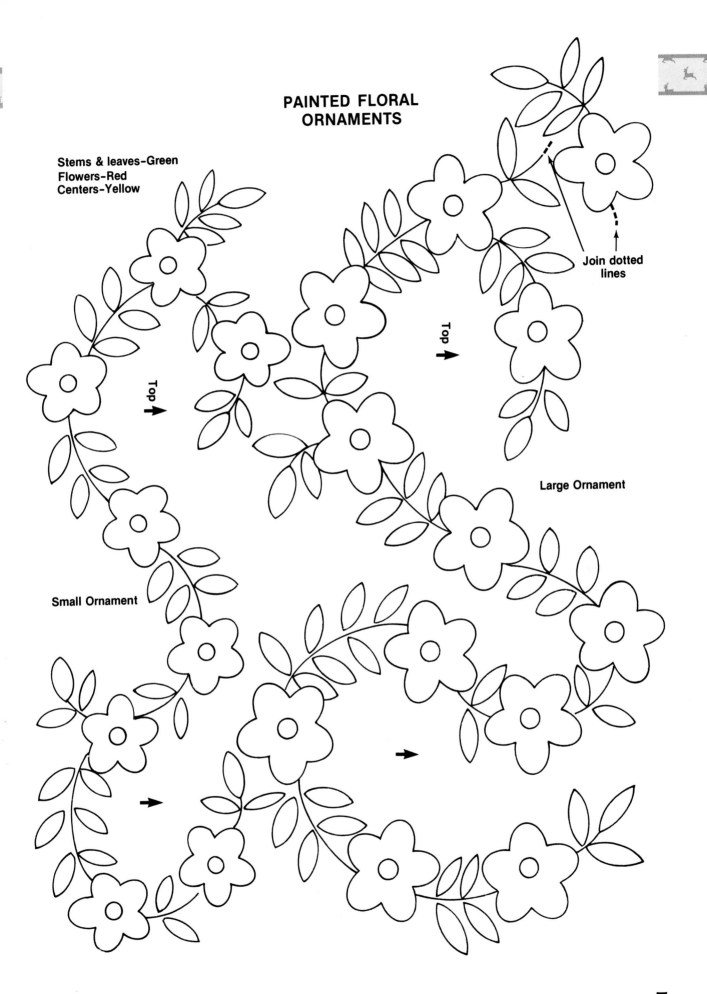

Join dotted lines

Top

Top

Large Ornament

Small Ornament

In colonial times, fresh fruit crafted into holiday trims symbolized a warm and generous spirit of hospitality. Inspired by those inviting arrangements, our lustrous fruit-bedecked wreath and ornaments will extend a cheerful welcome to your own loved ones and guests during the Christmas season.

You'll find it easy to stock your Christmas cupboard with these trims. They're made of glossy rattail cording wrapped and glued around plastic foam balls or a wreath, then coiled into fruit shapes and pinned into place.

Ornaments

MATERIALS

4-inch-diameter plastic foam balls
12-yard lengths of rattail cording in assorted colors
½-yard lengths of rattail for fruit and leaf shapes
Tape measure, fabric glue
Heavy interfacing
Metal florist hooks or paper clips for hangers
Silk pins, waxed paper

INSTRUCTIONS

Begin by wrapping a fabric tape measure around the center of a foam ball to find the center of the top and bottom. Mark each with a pin. For the hanger, dip the end of a metal florist hook or paper clip into glue and insert it into the center top of the ball.

Referring to the photograph for design ideas, wrap each ball with 12 yards of rattail cord. Spread a small amount of glue smoothly around the hook on top of the ball. Wrap the rattail around the hook and spiral it outward around the ball.

Continue covering the ball by gluing and wrapping small sections of the cord at a time. Allow the glue to dry before you work on the next section.

To change colors after wrapping part of the ball, cut the cord you are using at an angle; press the cut end firmly against the ball. Clip the end of the new cord, also at an angle; place it snugly against the first cord.

• **For fruit decorations:** Enlarge the patterns, *right*. Use small fruits for ornaments and large ones for a wreath.

Use interfacing to stabilize the fruit shapes. Trace the fruit patterns onto the interfacing. Lay the interfacing atop the waxed paper and lightly coat the motifs with glue. Working from the outside edges toward the center, coil a length of rattail in the appropriate color atop the glue.

When the shapes are covered with the cording, pull away the waxed paper; allow the rattail to dry. Then cut away any excess interfacing and pin fruits and leaves to the ornaments.

To form stems, use a toothpick to spread a thin line of glue on the ball. Press the cord into the glue. Except for the strawberries, glue the stems to the balls before you pin on the fruit. Add leaves after the fruit is glued to the ball.

For the watermelon "seeds," push black-headed pins into the fruit motif on the ornament.

Wreath

MATERIALS

14-inch-diameter foam wreath
61 yards of wine-colored rattail
30 yards of white rattail
½-yard lengths of rattail for fruit and leaf shapes
Fabric glue, interfacing
Silk pins, waxed paper

INSTRUCTIONS

Cut 23 eight-foot lengths of wine-colored cord. Tightly wrap and glue one length around the wreath, making a section. Add the next wine section ½ inch from the first one along the outer edge and ⅛ inch away along the inside edge (see diagram, *below*.) This leaves V-shaped sections empty for the white cord. Wrap 23 wine sections around the wreath.

Cut the white rattail into 48-inch lengths. Fill the V-shaped sections with white cord, slightly overlapping cords along the inner edge.

Make fruits and leaves according to the instructions for the ornaments. When dry, pin them to the wreath; add a hanger to the back.

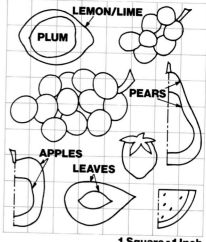

1 Square = 1 Inch

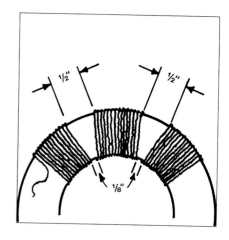

The stitched-in warmth of these delightful fabric ornaments goes hand in hand with the holiday spirit. You can hang the trims singly or clustered on your tree. Or, use them as attractive focal points on a wreath or colorful package.

The muslin and calico ornaments are adaptations of the traditional Cathedral Window quilt pattern. An easy-to-do folding and cutting sequence is the trick to creating these unusual 2-inch-square trims. For stocking stuffers, use the pattern for a pincushion or for a potpourri-filled sachet.

MATERIALS
Muslin (or other lightweight fabric) and calico scraps
Polyester fiberfill
Potpourri (optional)
Small red wooden beads
Thread

INSTRUCTIONS
Refer to the diagrams, *below*, to complete each step.

For each ornament, cut two 6½-inch squares from muslin or other lightweight fabric. Lay one square flat on your work surface, as shown in step 1.

Fold the square in half. Stitch across both short ends, using a ¼-inch seam allowance (step 2). Along the fold, clip to the end of the stitching; press the seams open. Repeat this step with the second muslin square.

Bring the ends of the seams together along the open edges. Stitch across the remaining raw edges, leaving an opening for turning (step 3). Repeat with the other square.

Turn squares right side out and slip-stitch openings closed (step 4). Press gently.

Fold corners of the squares to the center as shown in step 5 and pin them in place. Tack the corners at the center.

Hand-stitch the two squares together along one of the sides, as shown in step 6.

Fold the squares back to back and stitch them together along opposite side (step 7). You now have two folded squares that are stitched together along two edges and open at opposite ends.

Refold the tube in half, placing the seamed ends back to back, as shown in step 8. The diamond shape in the center becomes the window to frame the calico square.

Next, sew one of the open ends closed. Stuff the ornament with fiberfill, making a miniature "pillow." Or, fill the "pillow" with potpourri to make a sweet-smelling sachet. Stitch the ornament closed.

Finally, cut a calico square to fit the window; center and pin it in place. Roll the muslin edges of the window down around the raw edges of the calico and blindstitch them in place (step 9). Repeat this step for the other side of the ornament.

Add beads to the centers of the side edges of each "pillow" as shown in the photograph. Add a thread loop for hanging the ornament.

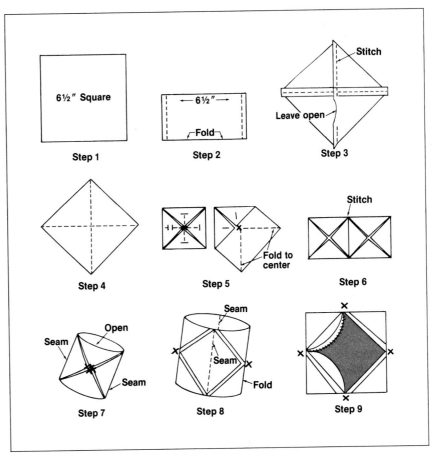

Crisp and festive—that's the beauty of these delicate snowflakes. Use them as trims on your holiday gifts to dress up even the plainest packages. Work a batch in threads or cords of differing weights so the sizes of the finished snowflakes vary, then hang them in a window to catch the winter sun. Or make enough of these lovely designs to trim your tree in lacy white.

We've included seven crocheted snowflakes and six macramed ones for you to make, so whether you're a beginner or an expert, you'll find a pattern that's just right for you. For example, among the crocheted snowflakes, pattern number four is worked entirely in chain stitches, except for the double crochet stitches worked in the ring to start the design. Even an inexperienced stitcher can complete it with ease.

If you're just getting started with macrame, the diagrams on page 15 will help you learn the basic knots.

Crocheted Ornaments

MATERIALS
Coats & Clark white Knit-Cro-Sheen (one ball makes several snowflakes), or substitute the thread of your choice (size of thread determines finished size of the design)
Size 7 steel crochet hook
Laundry starch
Straight pins

INSTRUCTIONS
Directions, *below,* correspond to the seven crocheted ornaments in the photograph as follows: Patterns one through five are shown left to right in the top shelf of the cabinet; patterns six and seven, left to right, are below the shelf.

To crochet the seven ornaments, follow the instructions for each pattern, referring to the crochet abbreviations on page 73.

When you have finished the snowflakes, mix a solution of heavy starch according to the manufacturer's instructions. Dip each snowflake into the solution until it is saturated.

Then, on a folded sheet or towel, pin each snowflake out to its symmetrical shape, using the photograph as a guide. Let the snowflakes dry away from heat and bright sunlight.

• **Pattern No. 1:** Ch 6; sl st to form ring. *Rnd 1:* Ch 4, * *yo twice; insert hook in ring, yo and draw up a lp, (yo and draw through 2 lps on hook) twice *. Rpt from * to *, yo and draw through all 3 lps on hook*—first cluster made; ch 5. Rpt from * to * 3 times, yo and draw through all 4 lps on hook—2nd cluster made; (ch 5, work cluster in ring) 4 times more; ch 5, join with sl st to top of first cluster—6 clusters made.

Rnd 2: * Ch 9, sl st in 5th ch *from hook*—picot made; (ch 7, sl st in 5th ch from hook) twice, (ch 5, sl st in 5th ch from hook) twice, sl st in same place where 3rd picot was made, (ch 7, sl st in 5th ch from hook) twice, *ch 4, sl st in top of same cluster*—spoke made, ch 3, sl st in 3rd ch of previous ch-5 lps; ch 4, sl st in same ch, ch 3, sl st in top of next cluster. Rpt from * around; join last ch-3 with sl st to base of first ch-9. Fasten off.

• **Pattern No. 2:** Ch 5; sl st to form ring. *Rnd 1:* Ch 8, dc in ring, * ch 5, dc in ring. Rpt from * around 3 times more; ch 5, sl st in 3rd ch of beg ch-8.

Rnd 2: * Sl st in each of first 3 ch of next ch-5, ch 6, sl st again in 3rd ch of ch-5, sl st in next 2 ch of ch-5, ch 1, sc in top of next dc. Rpt from * around 4 times, in next ch-5 make sl st in each of first 3 ch, ch 3, and tr in same ch as ch-3.

Rnd 3: Ch 7, tr in top of next dc, ch 6, sl st in top of tr just made, * ch 4, 3 dc in next ch-6 lp of previous rnd, ch 4, tr in top of next sc, ch 6, sl st in top of tr. Rpt from * around 4 times, ch 4, 2 dc in next ch-6 lp, sl st in 3rd ch of beg ch-7.

Rnd 4: * Ch 6, dc in next ch-6 lp, ch 6, sl st in top of dc just made, (ch 6, sl st in next dc) twice; ch 10, sl st in same dc, ch 6, sl st in next dc. Rpt from * around; join with sl st to base of first ch-6. Fasten off.

• **Pattern No. 3:** Ch 7; sl st to form ring. *Rnd 1:* Ch 4, 2 tr in ring, ch 3, * 3 tr in ring, ch 3. Rpt from * 4 times; join with sl st to 4th ch of beg ch-4.

Rnd 2: * Ch 5, *sl st in 3rd ch from hook*—picot made; ch 6, sl st in 3rd ch from hook to form 2nd picot, ch 2, sl st in top of 3rd tr, sl st in next ch-3 sp, ch 5, sl st in same ch-3 sp, sl st in top of next tr. Rpt from * around; join with sl st in beg sl st. Then cut the thread.

Continued

Snowflakes to Crochet & Macrame

Rnd 3: Attach thread to center of lp bet first and 2nd picots of previous rnd, * ch 6, sl st in 3rd ch from hook for picot, ch 15, sl st in same st as previous sl st, ch 8, sl st in 6th ch from hook, ch 10, sl st in same st as previous sl st, ch 5, sl st in 5th ch from hook, sl st in base of opposite picot, sl st in each of next 2 ch, ch 14, sl st in 14th ch from hook, ch 2, sl st in 2nd ch from hook, sl st in base of opposite picot, sl st in each of next 3 ch sts, sl st in same lp bet first and 2nd picots, ch 3, sc in next picot of previous rnd, ch 5, sl st in 4th ch from hook for picot, ch 2, sc in first picot on next lp of previous rnd, ch 3, sl st in center of lp. Rpt from * around; join with a sl st in beg sl st and fasten off.

• **Pattern No. 4:** Ch 8; sl st to form ring. *Rnd 1:* Ch 3, 17 dc in ring; join with sl st to top ch of ch-3 at beg of rnd.

Rnd 2: * Ch 7, sl st in 4th ch from hook for picot, (ch 6, sl st in 4th ch from hook) twice; ch 6, sl st in 6th ch from hook, ch 4, sl st in 4th ch from hook, (ch 6, sl st in 4th ch from hook) twice; ch 3, sl st in next dc, ch 3, sk 1 dc, sl st in next dc. Rpt from * around; join with sl st in dc at base of first ch-7. Fasten off.

• **Pattern No. 5:** Ch 8; sl st to form ring. *Rnd 1:* Ch 1, 15 sc in ring; join with sl st to ch-1. *Rnd 2:* * Ch 6, sc in next sc. Rpt from * around 14 times; ch 2, dc in same sp as beg ch-6—16 lps.

Rnd 3: * Ch 6, sk 1 lp, sc in next lp. Rpt from * around; ch 4, dc in same sp as first ch-6.

Rnd 4: * Ch 8, sl st in 4th ch from hook for picot, ch 6, sl st in 4th ch from hook for picot, ch 8, sc in 8th ch from hook, ch 4, sl st in 4th ch from hook, sc in base of opposite picot, sl st in next 2 ch, ch 4, sl st in 4th ch from hook, sc in base of opposite picot, ch 4, sc in next ch-6 lp. Rpt from * around; sl st in first sc. Fasten off.

• **Pattern No. 6:** Ch 5; sl st to form ring. *Rnd 1:* Ch 7, dc in ring, * ch 4, dc in ring. Rpt from * around 3 times; ch 4, join with sl st in 3rd ch of beg ch-7.

Rnd 2: * (Ch 5, holding last lp of each tr on hook make 2 tr in 5th ch from hook, yo and draw through all 3 lps at once—rice st made) twice; sc in top of next dc of previous rnd. Rpt from * around 5 times; join with sl st to base of first rice st.

Rnd 3: Ch 9, make rice st in 5th ch from hook, * ch 2, tr bet next 2 rice sts of previous rnd, (ch 4, sl st in 4th ch from hook for picot) 4 times, ch 9, sl st in 4th ch from hook for picot, (ch 4, sl st in 4th ch from hook for picot) 3 times, sl st in top of tr just made, ch 7, make a rice st in 5th ch from hook, tr in next sc of previous rnd, ch 5, make a rice st in 5th ch from hook. Rpt from * around; join with sl st in 4th ch of beg ch-9.

• **Pattern No. 7:** Ch 5; sl st to form ring. *Rnd 1:* Ch 1, * sc in ring, ch 5. Rpt from * around 5 times; join with sl st in first sc.

Rnd 2: Sl st in each of the first 2 sts of first ch-5 lp, in next st make sl st, ch 1, sc, * ch 7, sl st in 3rd ch from hook to make first picot, ch 3, sl st in same st used to make first picot, ch 3, sl st in 3rd ch from hook, sl st in base of first picot—picot cluster made;

ch 4, sc in 3rd ch of next ch-5 lp. Rpt from * around; ending with sl st in first sc of rnd.

Rnd 3: * Ch 13, sl st in 7th ch from hook, ch 8, sl st in 6th ch from hook, ch 10, sl st in same st used for last sl st, ch 6, sl st in 6th ch from hook, sl st in same st used to form last 2 lps, sl st in next 2 ch sts, sl st in base of opposite lp, ch 6, sl st in same st as last sl st, sl st in each of next 6 ch, sl st in base of ch-13, ch 9, tr in center picot of picot cluster, ch 10, sl st in top of tr, ch 10, sl st in 10th ch from hook, sl st again in top of tr, ch 9, sl st in next sc of previous rnd.

Rpt from * around; join with sl st in base of first ch-13. Fasten off.

Macrame Ornaments

MATERIALS
Coats and Clark white Knit-Cro-Sheen (one ball makes dozens of ornaments)
½-inch-diameter bone rings
Craft glue; waxed paper
Transparent acrylic spray

INSTRUCTIONS
The six macrame patterns, *opposite,* correspond to the photograph on page 13 as follows: Pattern number one is the snowflake in the center of the back row. Designs two through

six are arranged clockwise around pattern number one.

Following the directions below for each ornament, mount the required number of threads on a bone ring, using a lark's head knot (below). Then work the pattern as required for each snowflake.

When you have tied all of the knots in a snowflake, place a drop of glue on the last knot to secure it; let dry.

To form a hanging loop, clip all but two threads at the outside edge of the last knot. Overlap the remaining two threads ½ inch from the ends and glue them together.

When the glue is dry, place the snowflakes on waxed paper and saturate them with clear acrylic spray. When dry, turn the snowflakes over and coat again with acrylic.

• **Pattern No. 1:** Mount twenty-four 18-inch-long threads onto a ring. Divide the threads into 12 four-thread groups and tie a square knot with each group adjacent to the ring. (To tie a square knot, see the diagram, *below*.) Tie a second square knot above the first to form a small circle, looping outside threads so that circles are interlaced. Tie five square knots above each circle. Tie another square knot, making a circle the same size as the first circles made. (See the photograph, page 13.) Glue.

• **Pattern No. 2:** Mount twenty-four 12-inch-long threads onto a ring. Divide the threads into 12 four-thread groups. Tie two square knots so that each knot is adjacent to the ring. With two threads from adjacent knots, form 12 new four-thread groups, then tie a square knot with each group.

Divide the 12 four-thread groups into six alternating groups. With every other group, tie one square knot to form a long, narrow loop. With the remaining groups, form two small circles with two square knots (see photograph). Glue.

• **Pattern No. 3:** Mount twelve 12-inch-long threads onto the ring. Divide threads into 6 four-thread groups. With each group, tie one square knot adjacent to the ring. Tie a second knot on the same groups of threads to form a small circle (see photograph).

Now divide the threads into six new groups of four threads (using two threads from adjacent circles). Tie a square knot with each new group of threads and a second square knot forming another small circle (see photograph). Glue.

• **Pattern No. 4:** Mount twenty 18-inch-long threads onto a ring. Divide the threads into 20 two-thread groups. With each group, tie five alternating half hitches (see the diagram, *below*). Then connect the four threads of two adjacent sinnets (groups of knots) with a square knot to form 10 elongated loops (see the photograph).

Keeping all the work flat, take two threads from two adjacent loops to form 10 new four-thread groups. Then tie a square knot. Tie a sinnet of four alternating half hitches on the two strands above each square knot. Form a circle with these by connecting the two strands with a square knot. Glue. (This design requires shaping just after spraying.)

• **Pattern No. 5:** Mount fourteen 18-inch-long threads onto a ring. Divide the threads into 7 four-thread groups. With each group, tie a sinnet of three square knots adjacent to the ring. Divide threads into seven new groups of four threads (using two threads from adjacent knots). Tie a square knot.

Working with the same four-thread group, tie another square knot below the ones just made, forming a circle (see photograph). Tie four alternating half hitches on two of the two-thread groups above each of the square knots. Join the adjacent strands with a square knot; secure with glue.

• **Pattern No. 6:** Mount fourteen 12-inch-long threads onto a ring. Divide the threads into 7 four-thread groups. Then, with each group, tie one square knot adjacent to the ring. Divide the threads into seven new groups of four threads each (using two threads each from the adjacent knots). Tie a square knot with each group.

Divide the threads into the same four-thread groups as before and tie three square knots over the threads. Glue.

Lark's Head Knot

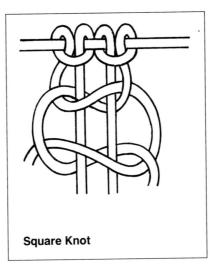

Square Knot

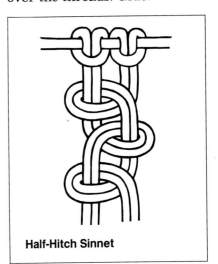

Half-Hitch Sinnet

As sweet and old-fashioned as high-buttoned shoes, these cross-stitched medallions are crafted of delicate lace and silky floss in a palette of soft pastels. The result is a bevy of birds, butterflies, and flowers that will warm the hearts of all the romantics among your family and friends.

These three favorite designs from nature also make charming package trims and holiday mementos. Stuff them with fiberfill and give them with pride to special folks on your Christmas list to use as pincushions.

Or, tuck in a pinch of scented potpourri or a few rose petals when you stitch the medallions, and present your friends with sweet-smelling sachets they can enjoy long after Christmas is over.

MATERIALS

For each ornament:

6-inch square of No. 26-count even-weave linen

Embroidery floss in the colors listed in the color key, *below right*

12 inches of 1-inch-wide lace

3-inch-diameter fabric circle for the back

2½-inch-diameter circle of art foam (available at art supply stores)

5 inches of gold braid

Needle, thread

INSTRUCTIONS

To begin an ornament, stay-stitch ½ inch from the raw edges of the linen square to prevent the fabric from raveling.

To embroider the ornaments, use two strands of floss. Keep the stitches uniform by working them in the same direction over two threads of the linen. Follow the diagrams, *right*, to work the border design, then stitch the nature motifs.

To assemble each ornament, trim the embroidered front to 3 inches in diameter. Place the front and back together, wrong sides facing. Then blindstitch the back to the front, using a ¼-inch seam allowance. Tuck in the raw edges as you go.

When you have sewn about halfway around the ornament, slip an art foam circle between the front and back layers of fabric, then finish blindstitching. The foam will pad the ornament and help it maintain its circular shape.

For the finishing touch, fold the lace in half lengthwise and blindstitch it to the edge of the ornament. Tack a gold braid hanging loop to the back.

If you like, adapt the designs to small gift items, or experiment with different colors of floss. For suggestions on how to choose pleasing color combinations, see pages 62-63.

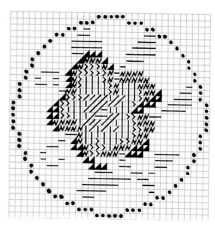

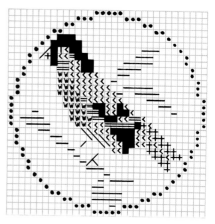

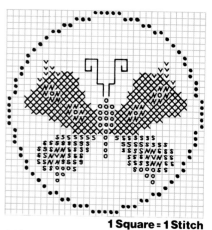

1 Square = 1 Stitch

COLOR KEY:

⊙	Dk. brown	⊡	Dk. violet
⊠	Lt. brown	⋈	Violet
■	Brown	⊠	Lt. jade
⊞	White	⑤	Dk. jade
⧄	Yellow	⊞	Tan
⊳	Pink	⋈	Grey
⋈	Rose	⋈	Dk. grey
◪	Red	⊟	Blue
⊟	Green		

16

Inspired by the rich colors and elegant detail found in Renaissance paintings, this stitch-and-stuff angel is a radiant ornament to top your Christmas tree.

We've included a full-size pattern for the front of the angel (on pages 20-21). Just trace it onto the fabric, add color with paints, markers, or fabric crayons, and embellish with embroidery, beads, and other trims, making the angel as simple or as lavish as you prefer.

MATERIALS

⅜ yard of closely woven white cotton fabric

Dressmaker's carbon paper and tracing wheel

Permanent, fine-tip brown marking pen

Acrylic or fabric paints in iridescent gold and copper, yellow, pink, and lavender (or colors of your choice)

Sable paintbrush

Embroidery floss in brown, dark blue, and light and dark greens

Embroidery needle and hoop

Clear, gold, and dark blue beads; thread to match

Polyester fiberfill or potpourri for sachet

INSTRUCTIONS

For the front view of the angel, trace the full-size pattern on pages 20-21. Transfer it to fabric using light-colored dressmaker's carbon and a tracing wheel or pencil. Or, tape fabric to a window with the pattern behind it; trace the design onto the fabric. Mark a stitching line ¼ inch beyond the outline of the angel, and allow a ½-inch seam margin all around. (Do not cut the fabric yet.)

You can make an angel with the design on the front only. For the back design, enlarge the pattern, *right*; transfer it to the fabric following the directions given above.

Trace over all design lines with a brown marking pen.

Complete any painting or decorative stitching before you cut out and assemble the angel. Instructions follow for the angel shown, but feel free to experiment with the techniques and colors you prefer.

• *Painting:* Use quality artists' acrylic paints or paints specially made for working on fabric. To begin, place a small amount of paint on a glass plate; thin with water until mixture is the consistency of light cream. To lighten colors, add a drop of white paint to a few drops of water; mix in a color.

If necessary, add a few more drops of water to lighten the overall effect; don't add more white or the colors will look chalky on the fabric.

Use iridescent gold paint for the wings, cuffs, and the flowers and trim around the bottom of the dress. Use copper paint for the halo and trumpet. Paint the hair yellow, the dress pink, and the sash lavender. (See the photograph for guidance.)

Before painting, lay the fabric over a large sheet of cardboard padded with layers of newspaper or paper towels. Tape or pin the fabric to the cardboard so that it is smooth and taut. Dip a small brush into the paint and remove excess water by lightly daubing the brush on a paper towel or the edge of a plate.

To prevent paint from bleeding on the fabric, do not overload the brush. Paint *up to but not over* the brown outlines; leave a sliver of unpainted fabric between colors to keep them from running together. Paint large areas of color first, letting each painted area dry before moving on to an adjacent area.

Try to use a light wash of color or so that the outlines and details remain clear. If you make a mistake, dab at the paint with a wet tissue. If this does not remove the mistake, brush a bit of white paint over the mistake and, when dry, paint the correct color on top.

When the painted angel is dry, set the colors by pressing the wrong side of the fabric with a warm iron. If you wish, spray-starch the fabric lightly as you press to give it extra body.

• *Embroidery:* Use touches of embroidery to highlight the design. For best results, limit the stitchery to important details, such as the halo, trims, flowers, and facial features, rather than trying for an overall embroidered effect.

Using a single strand of black or brown embroidery thread, work the facial features in stem (or outline) stitches. Use cotton or silk floss, metallic thread, pearl cotton, and a variety of simple embroidery stitches to embellish the angel's dress, hair, and trumpet.

For our angel, we stitched the olive branch in satin stitches using light and dark greens. The facial features are worked in brown outline stitches, and the small dots around the flowers and other details on the dress are blue French knots.

• *Beads and sequins:* If desired, embellish the wings, halo, and dress with small beads, seed pearls, sequins, or glass jewels. Especially suitable are clear, gold, and tinted seed beads; iridescent and colored sequins; star sequins; bugle beads; and rocaille beads.

Continued

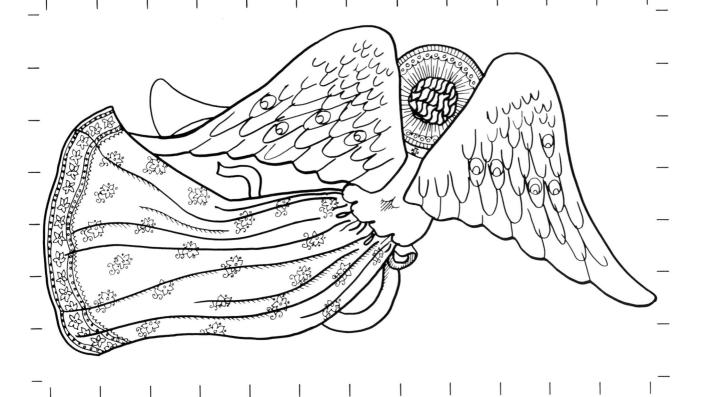

1 Square = 1 Inch

Elegant Beaded Angel

We used clear and opalescent beads scattered on the angel's wings, gold beads in the halo, and blue beads in the centers of the flowers on the dress.

The following techniques also work well for decorating the treetop angel.

• *Colored pencils:* High-quality colored pencils or artists' oil pencils yield beautiful results on this angel. They're easy to use, and their colors can be delicate or strong depending on the amount of pressure you use.

After coloring, lay fabric facedown over several paper towels. Place additional paper towels atop the fabric; press with a warm iron to set the colors.

• *Permanent fabric markers:* Be careful to select fine-tip fabric markers that do not bleed on the fabric or make the brown outlines run. To test your pens, lightly mark scrap fabric; check to see if the ink runs.

Because the inks in permanent marking pens often look dark when applied to fabric, choose soft, subtle shades. Use a light touch so colors won't overwhelm the angel's fine details. Be careful not to obliterate the brown outlines by coloring over them. To set colors, press the angel with a warm iron on the wrong side of the fabric.

• *Quilting:* After all other decorating is complete, you may trapunto quilt portions of the angel to give details of the design a bit of extra dimension when the angel is stuffed. Pin a piece of muslin, organdy, or other lightweight backing to the wrong side of the fabric. Quilt along the design lines you wish to emphasize, such as the angel's sash or around her halo.

After quilting, use small scissors to carefully cut a slit in the *backing fabric only.* Tuck a bit of fiberfill or a few strands of soft, light-colored yarn into the pocket between the backing and top fabrics, then whipstitch the edges of the slit closed.

Instead of trapunto quilting, you may quilt along the design lines in the traditional manner to add subtle overall texture to the angel. Place pieces of batting and backing fabric under the angel and baste the three layers together. Then stretch

the layers in an embroidery hoop and quilt with tiny running stitches along lines in the wings, folds of the dress, halo, or other areas of emphasis.

When the angel is completely quilted, remove the basting. Trim the batting and backing close to the quilting so that they don't catch in the seam allowance when you sew the angel together.

Assembling the angel

Cut out the decorated front and back of the angel ¾ inch beyond the solid outline. With right sides facing, pin and baste front and back sides together, matching solid outlines.

Sew the angel together by hand or machine, stitching ¼ inch outside the solid outline and following curves as closely as possible. Leave an opening at the base of the angel for turning and stuffing. Trim the seams; clip curves and corners up to the seam line. Notch the seam allowance if necessary so the angel will be shaped correctly when turned.

Turn the angel right side out, gently maneuvering the curves and corners into place with a knitting needle.

Stuff the angel with small pieces of fiberfill, starting at the head and working across. Avoid overstuffing the angel to keep the shape from becoming puckered and distorted. Turn under raw edges along the base; slipstitch the opening closed. To hang the angel, attach a loop of nylon thread or ribbon.

To create sweet-smelling sachets, fill the angel with potpourri mix. To make a mix, clip rose petals during summer and dry them in a shady, well-ventilated place. Store the petals in an airtight container, stirring them every few days.

Crush a mixture of lavender, orrisroot, tonka bean, sandalwood, lemon verbena, frankincense, and myrrh until you get a pleasing scent combination. Mix these herbs with the petals; cure the mixture covered for about six weeks, stirring often.

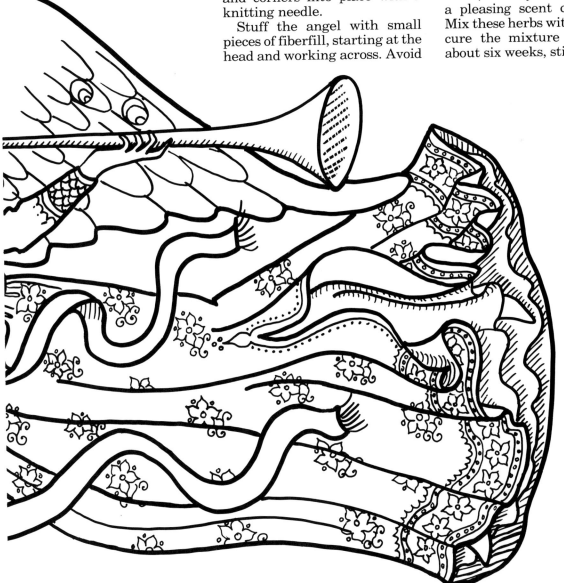

Small touches—when they're just right—can make your whole house say "Merry Christmas." So we've gathered pillows, trims, and other accessories to help you celebrate the season throughout your home.

Festive projects like these appliquéd pillows are a warm complement to your traditional stockings and wreaths. The special joy you'll find in crafting them will spruce up your Christmas spirits as well as your home. Instructions for this trio of patchwork pillows begin on the next page.

Show off your patchwork and quilting skills with the holiday pillows shown on pages 22-23. Propped on a sofa, bed, or hearth, these bright pillows spread the spirit of Christmas all through the house.

MATERIALS

(For all three pillows)
Fabrics in the following amounts and colors: 3 yards of white cotton; 1¾ yards of green polka dot; 1 yard of red polka dot; ½ yard of solid green; ¼ yard each of light and dark green Christmas calicos
Scraps of three light and two dark Christmas calicos, and brown cotton
White embroidery floss
5½ yards of gathered 1½-inch-wide lace or eyelet
Three 18-inch squares of quilt batting
Three 16-inch pillow forms
White, green, and red thread
4 yards of white ball fringe
Two white flower appliqués

INSTRUCTIONS

• **General directions:** For each pillow, cut two 17-inch squares from white fabric. Enlarge the patterns, *right*; pieces include ¼-inch seam margins. Press under the seam allowances, then pin and whipstitch the appliqués into place.

To quilt a pillow top, sandwich the batting between the top and second white square. Baste the layers together and quilt as desired.

For the ruffle on each pillow, cut three 6x45-inch strips from red or green polka dot fabric. With right sides facing, sew the ends of strips together to form a circle. Fold lengthwise, wrong sides facing. Gather along raw edges to fit pillow top. Sew lace

or eyelet to ruffle. With right sides together, matching raw edges, stitch ruffle to quilted pillow top.

For the back, cut two 12x17-inch white fabric pieces. Hem one long side on each piece. Pin backs to pillow top, right sides together, overlapping the backs to fit. Stitch, securing ruffle in the seam. Turn right side out and insert pillow form.

• **Holly wreath pillow** (*at left in photograph*): Enlarge wreath patterns A and B, *below*. Cut nine leaves each from the green polka dot, two green calicos, and solid green fabric. Cut one red polka dot bow.

In the center of one white square, draw a 10½-inch-diameter circle. Referring to photograph for placement, pin leaves around the circle; pin bow at bottom of wreath. Whipstitch pieces in place. Using white floss and outline stitches, embroider the bow, following the dashed lines on the pattern.

Quilt the appliquéd top and finish the pillow, following the general directions.

• **Branched Christmas tree pillow** (*in center of photograph*): Enlarge branched tree patterns

A through F, *below*. Referring to the photograph for fabric colors, cut two each of A through D, one each of E and F.

Turn under seam allowance along curved sides of A through D, all around E, and on sides and bottom of F. Arrange pieces on white square, lapping each branch over the one below and inserting ball fringe under lower edges of the branches; stitch. Tack floral appliqué to treetop.

Quilt top and finish pillow, following general directions.

• **Scalloped Christmas tree pillow** (*at right in photograph*): Enlarge the scalloped tree patterns A through F, *below*. With dotted lines along fold of fabric, cut one of each piece, referring to the photograph for fabrics.

Turn under seam allowance and baste around sides and bottom of A, B, and C; all around D and E; and on sides of F.

Lapping each scalloped section over the one below, pin pieces to white square. Insert ball fringe under the scallops. Whipstitch the pieces in place. Tack lace along top of tree base and floral appliqué to treetop.

Quilt top and finish pillow, following general directions.

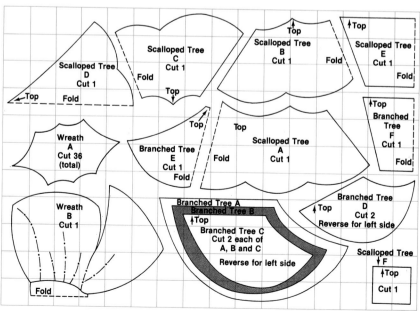

1 Square = 1 Inch

Cheery Cross-Stitch Towel

As appealing as fresh-baked cookies or brightly wrapped gifts, this cross-stitched guest towel offers a heartfelt greeting to your holiday visitors.

Because of its rectangular border, this merry motif is not just for towels—it's also fitting for pillowcases, stockings, apron bibs, place mats, or any holiday project that calls for an extra-festive touch.

To create an array of homespun sentiments, you can adapt other seasons greetings, such as "JOY" or "PEACE," to cross-stitch, using our Noel pattern as a guide.

MATERIALS
15x24 inches of off-white evenweave hardanger or Aida cloth
Green and red embroidery floss or pearl cotton
Embroidery needle and hoop
Green and red colored pencils
Graph paper
Off-white thread

INSTRUCTIONS
Using colored pencils, transfer the charts, *below right,* to graph paper. Complete the rows of decorative motifs by repeating the border designs on the "N" pattern. Insert the remaining letters within the decorative borders. (Refer to the photograph for guidance.)

To begin, locate the center of one short edge of the fabric and measure 1½ inches in from the edge. Using three strands of embroidery floss, begin stitching at this point, counting the threads carefully. On hardanger cloth, work stitches over two threads; on Aida cloth, over one thread.

Work the border lines that enclose the bottom row of motifs, then complete the design across the towel, following the chart and color key.

To finish the towel, turn up narrow hems, or hem the sides only and fringe the last ½ inch of the ends.

If you wish to adapt other sentiments to cross-stitch, first chart your design on graph paper. As you determine the width of the borders and letters, keep in mind the size of the project on which you will stitch the motif. To vary the borders, experiment with simple holiday shapes such as bells, stars, and Christmas trees.

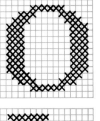

1 Square = 1 Stitch

COLOR KEY
- ■ Green
- ⊠ Red
- ⊡ Red French Knot

25

Inspired by a Christmas song, this quilted wall hanging is appliquéd with a delightful partridge in a pear tree. For an extra-festive touch, adorn your mantel with painted wooden versions of the quilt's pear, heart, and bird motifs.

The size of the finished quilt is 33x42 inches.

MATERIALS
3 yards of green calico
1 yard of unbleached muslin
8-inch square of tan and red gingham
½ yard of yellow fabric
¼ yard of green fabric
Scraps of red, red print, tan, tan print, and brown fabric
Embroidery floss, thread
35x44 inches of quilt batting
Embroidery hoop
Green bias tape

INSTRUCTIONS
From muslin fabric, cut a 27½x33¾-inch rectangle and four 4½-inch squares for corners. From green calico, cut two 4½x24½-inch side borders and two 4½x33¾-inch strips for top and bottom borders.

Using ¼-inch seams, stitch side borders to the sides of background. Sew squares to the ends of top and bottom borders; sew to the sides and background.

To shape arc along the top, pencil in the curve on border strip. Stay-stitch along this line. Clip through the seam allowance to the stitching. Turn under seam allowance and press. Hand-stitch the arc portion of border to the background, referring to pattern for guidance.

Appliqué a narrow strip of green bias tape over seam lines around muslin background.

Enlarge the pattern, *below,* onto graph paper. Use this as a master pattern for the placement of the appliqués. To make patterns for the individual appliqués, trace the shapes onto tissue paper.

Cut pieces, adding a ¼-inch seam allowance all around. Cut tree from green calico, pot from tan and red gingham, hearts from red and red print, pears from yellow fabric, and leaves from green fabric. Cut pieces for bird, trunk, and ribbon from colors indicated on the pattern.

On each shape, turn under a seam allowance; press, baste. *Note:* To shape curved appliqués, cut typing paper to the size the appliqué will be when stitched. Place on wrong side of appliqué. Fold seam allowance over paper; baste. Press well; remove basting and paper.

Referring to the master pattern, pin appliqués in place, then blindstitch around edges.

Using 3 strands of floss, outline-stitch the lettering and stitch around all shapes, using floss that contrasts with the fabrics (see photograph).

From green calico, cut a backing the same size as quilt top. Sandwich batting between top and backing. Baste. To quilt, place basted quilt in frame or hoop. Use white quilting thread and tiny running stitches.

Quilt ⅛ inch beyond edges of border and corner pieces; outline quilt around appliqués. To fill in background, quilt graceful lines around design motifs, spacing rows approximately 1 inch apart (see the photograph).

Bind raw edges with green bias tape. Add calico bows to the corners, if desired.

To hang quilt, sew curtain rings or a 3-inch-wide muslin strip (with ½ inch turned under on each long edge) to top of quilt back. Insert a rod through rings or muslin channel; hang.

Or, use strips of Velcro fastening tape to attach quilt to a wooden frame or board so you can hang it from a single nail.

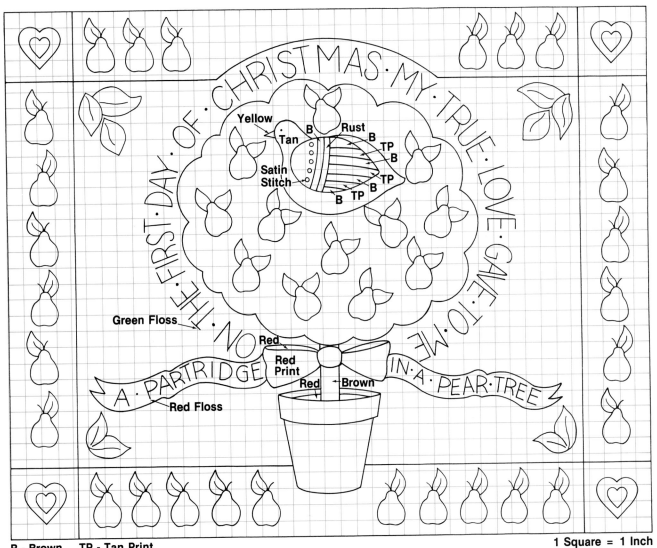

B - Brown   TP - Tan Print

1 Square = 1 Inch

Fantasy Father Christmas

Though modeled after the Father Christmas of centuries past, this charming soft-sculpture figure has all the kindly qualities of today's jolly old elf. With his bright red cloak, long white beard, and a bag of toys slung over his shoulder, the 10-inch-high figure will make a merry accent for your holiday home.

MATERIALS

⅜ yard of red velour
⅜ yard of white cotton fabric
6x10 inches of brown suede-type knit fabric
Scraps of tan nylon hosiery
Polyester fiberfill
Two black seed beads for eyes
8-inch-tall plastic foam cone
9 inches of No. 16 florist's wire
1 yard of ½-inch-wide white fake fur
White unspun wool fiber (available at stores that sell weaving supplies) for hair, beard, and eyebrows
Tassel or bell for hat
Scraps of yarn
Scraps of quilt batting
Narrow cord for belt and bag
Light brown thread and needle
Hair spray, powdered blusher

INSTRUCTIONS

The Santa's head and arms are shaped from nylon and fiberfill, and the body is fashioned from a foam cone base. Create the soft-sculpture Santa by following these instructions for each part of the figure.

• *Head:* Place a ball of fiberfill that is about 2 inches in diameter in the center of a 5-inch square of nylon. Gather the nylon around the fiberfill and tie it off with yarn to form the head. Think of the tied-off area as the neck (Figure 1, *right*).

• *Nose:* Insert a single-threaded needle through the back of the head and out the front at a point about halfway down the face. Shape the face as much as possible by using the point of the needle to fluff up the stuffing where the nose and cheeks will be.

Form the bridge of the nose by pinching a ¼-inch-wide vertical ridge in the middle of the face. Insert the needle at the top of one side of the nose; come out on the other side of the ridge.

To hold the shape of the nose, stitch back and forth horizontally through the stuffing for the length of the nose (about ⅜ inch). The stitches will be hidden under the ridge of the nylon and fiberfill. Make the stitches slightly farther apart as you reach the nostrils (Figure 2).

When you reach the bottom of the ridge, poke and lift the end of the nose with the needle.

To form each nostril, make a semicircle of small running stitches through the surface of the face. Begin at the bottom of the ridge and stitch down and around to the middle of the nose (Figure 3).

Next, stitch from the center of the nostril back to the corner where you began the running stitches. Insert your needle into the head at that point. Then pull the thread gently and secure it at the back of the head where it will be covered by the hair and hat. Repeat for the other nostril.

• *Eyes:* Form eye sockets by taking a stitch from under the hairline to a point about ¼ inch on each side of the stitches that formed the top of the nose. Pull your stitches tightly to the back of the head until indentations form, then secure. Sew a seed bead in each eye socket.

• *Mouth:* Bring the needle from the back of the head to a point directly under one eye, about ¼ inch below one nostril. Make a curved line of running stitches through the surface of the face to a similar point under the other eye. Pull gently and secure the thread under the hairline.

To form a smile, take a stitch from under the hairline to one corner of the mouth. Stitch through the stuffing toward the outside corner of the eye and out the back of the head. Pull gently to turn up the corner of the mouth. Secure the stitch; repeat on the other side.

• *Eyebrows:* With white or invisible thread, tack a few short strands of unspun wool fiber in an arc over the eyes.

Continued

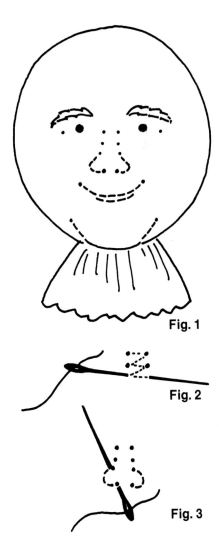

Fig. 1

Fig. 2

Fig. 3

Fantasy Father Christmas

• *Arms and hands:* Cut out two 1¼x5½-inch pieces of nylon. Fold each piece in half lengthwise and, with scissors, round off one end of each for the hand.

Beginning at the rounded end, overcast the edges using small, closely spaced stitches. Continue overcasting to a point about 1 inch up the arm from the rounded end. Turn the arm inside out and stuff the hand.

Pinch about one third of the hand into a ridge for the thumb. Using the same technique you used to hold the shape of the nose, stitch back and forth horizontally to form the thumb. For fingers, divide the remainder of the hand in half, then in half again, so that the fingers are about even in size. Mark these divisions with pins.

Working from front to back, stitch through the hand along the division lines. Repeat this procedure for the other hand.

To shape the arms, bend each end of the florist's wire into a small circle. Wrap a scrap of batting around the entire wire; secure with stitches. Insert padded wire into the stuffed hands; hand-stitch the rest of the nylon arms together around the padded wire. The finished length of the arms, fingertip to fingertip, should be about 11 inches.

• *Body:* Form the base of the body by wrapping the cone with white fabric. Stitch to secure.

With a rubber band, fasten the head to the covered cone. Securely backstitch the head to the fabric on the cone. Then remove the rubber band and replace the yarn tied around the neck with thread.

Position the arms across the top back of the cone so that the thumbs point up. Then, across the back of the figure, securely stitch the arms to the cloth on the cone. Bend the arms to the front, turning one arm up and the other toward the waist.

Pad the figure's upper torso and shoulders by tacking scraps of batting or fiberfill to the white fabric. Slip a piece of nylon over the upper torso; stitch into place.

• *Cloak:* Enlarge the pattern, *below right,* by flopping the design along the fold lines. Pay close attention to the cutting lines for the neckline. Adding a ¼-inch seam allowance, cut the cloak from red velour.

Fold the cloak, right sides together; stitch side seams. Slit cloak along center front from the neckline to the bottom.

With the right sides together, turn up ¼ inch on the sleeves, the bottom edge of the cloak, and the slit edges of the front; press and stitch. Hand-stitch a strip of ½-inch-wide "fur" to the bottom and sleeves, and down *one* side of the front.

Slip the cloak on the figure. Lap the fur-trimmed edge of the front over other side; tack in place. Tie a cord belt around the figure's waist.

• *Hat:* Enlarge the hat pattern, *right,* flopping it as indicated and adding a ¼-inch seam allowance along the slanted edge. Cut the hat from red velour.

Fold the hat, right sides together, along the fold line and stitch along the edge to which you added the seam allowance. Along remaining raw edge, fold up ¼ inch, right sides together. Trim with fur. Fold back the point of the hat and tack down with a tassel or bell.

• *Beard and hair:* Arrange unspun wool to form the beard and hair. If the head has become flat from handling, shape it by fluffing up the stuffing with the point of the needle. Tack the beard and hair to the head with white or transparent thread. Spray with hair spray.

Lightly apply blusher to the figure's cheeks and to the tip of his nose. Then secure the hat in place with straight pins hidden under the fur.

• *Bag:* On the piece of suede-type fabric, fold over 1 inch of one long edge (wrong sides together). Then topstitch ⅛ and ¼ inches from the fold.

Fold the bag in half, right sides together, so that the folded top edges are facing. With scissors, round off the bottom edges. Stitch the bag together along the bottom and side using a ¼-inch seam allowance. Turn the bag right side out.

Make ties for the bag by using a blunt needle to thread a 12-inch piece of cord through the channel at the top of the bag. At each end, pierce the channel to bring the cord to the outside.

Loosely stuff the bottom of the bag with fiberfill. Pull the cord to partially close the bag; tie the ends together. Hang the bag over the figure's shoulder and stitch the upturned hand around the ends of the cord.

To the inside and outside of the top of the bag, attach miniature dolls, books, wrapped gifts, instruments, and other novelties. Tuck a Christmas tree under the figure's other arm. Then make a scroll listing "Good boys and girls" and pin it to his hand.

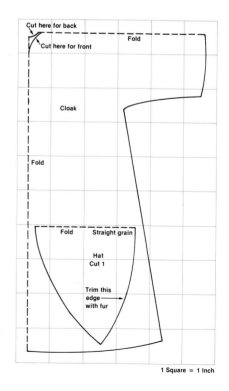

1 Square = 1 Inch

With European charm and old-world flavor, this delightful needlepoint design depicts a classic scene from Christmases past.

The candlelit tree and children's old-fashioned dress suggest a Christmas Eve celebration of long ago. But as any family knows, the image of laughing children playing beneath the tree is truly timeless.

Such a special design deserves an elegant finishing touch. If you wish, set off the needlepoint with a gilded frame and display it in a place of honor during the holiday season.

Or, stitch the canvas into a cover for a photograph album to preserve cherished memories of your own glowing Christmas trees and merry holiday gatherings.

Continued

Holiday Dance in Needlepoint

MATERIALS

16x18 inches of No. 12 mono needlepoint canvas

3-ply Persian needlepoint yarns in ecru and the colors listed in the color key, *below right*

Needlepoint frame or artists' stretcher strips

No. 20 blunt needle

INSTRUCTIONS

To determine the amounts of yarn needed for this project, consult your local yarn shop. You may wish to use appropriate colored yarns left over from other projects.

To keep the needlepoint canvas from raveling as you work, tape or hem the edges. Mount the canvas on a needlepoint frame or on wooden stretcher strips to avoid distortion and to make blocking the finished piece easier.

To begin, find the vertical center of the canvas by counting threads or measuring with a ruler. The center thread will be one of the two vertical rows that form the treetop.

Use two strands of Persian yarn and basket-weave stitches throughout the design. Following the chart, *opposite*, first stitch the darkest portions of the Christmas tree. Next, work the lightest areas of the tree branches. Fill in the remainder of the tree areas with the appropriate shades of yarn.

Continue to follow the chart to work the tree decorations, candles, and the dancing children. Work three French knots in medium yellow on the front of the boy's vest.

When the central motif is completed, stitch the border design. Finish working the piece by filling in the background with ecru yarn.

Remove the canvas from the frame and block it to eliminate any distortion that may have occurred from the tension and pull of the stitches.

• **To block the canvas:** First cut a piece of ½-inch plywood to a size that will easily accommodate the finished needlepoint. Attach a piece of quilt batting to the board, then cover it with high-quality gingham fabric, keeping the grain of the fabric as straight as possible.

Dampen the canvas and, with rustproof T-pins, mount it to the board. Follow the gingham squares to align the corners and edges of the canvas.

Sprinkle the canvas with water and let it dry at least 24 hours. Then remove the canvas from the board and press it lightly on the back side with a warm iron.

• **To frame the needlepoint:** Mount the canvas on a plywood board the size of the finished needlework. Pad the board with batting. Stretch the needlepoint over the board and staple it to the back.

Cut and assemble a molding for the frame, or take the needlepoint to a local framer for professional finishing.

• **To make an album cover:** On brown paper, draw a rectangle the length of the cover and the width of the book's circumference (from flap to flap), adding a ½-inch seam allowance. Draw another rectangle the length and width of the *front* cover, adding seam allowances.

From linen, wool, or other sturdy fabric, cut two shapes for each rectangle. From batting, cut one long rectangle. Hem one long side on each of the smaller fabric rectangles.

To create pocket flaps: With right sides facing and raw edges matching, baste one hemmed rectangle to the end of one large rectangle. Repeat with the other hemmed rectangle.

Lay the batting so it is flat and smooth. On top of the batting, lay the large rectangle with the two hemmed pieces so that the small rectangles are faceup. Then lay the remaining large rectangle on top with the wrong side faceup.

Stitch the three layers together around all four sides, leaving one short side open. Clip corners, turn to right side, and press. Slip-stitch opening closed.

With the cover right side up, lightly draw a rectangle on the front cover where you want the needlepoint to be. *In the top layer of fabric only,* cut an opening that is ½ inch smaller than the rectangle. Clip diagonally to the corners of the rectangle; fold under the raw edges.

Insert the needlepoint under the cover and slip-stitch it to the cover fabric. Insert the album into the pocket flaps.

COLOR KEY

- ■ Dark Green
- ⊠ Medium Green
- ⊡ Light Green
- ◪ Black
- ▲ Light Shade of Sole of Shoe
- ▼ Dark Shade of Sole of Shoe
- ▢ Flesh Color
- ◎ Darker Flesh Color
- Ⓢ Dark Red
- ◪ Medium Dark Red
- ◹ Red
- ⊞ Orange-Red
- ⊟ Light Orange-Red
- ◫ Dark Blue
- ▽ Medium Blue
- ▬ Medium Gray
- ℕ Light Gray
- ⊡ White
- ⊞ Dark Brown
- ◿ Light Brown
- ▮ Medium Yellow
- ⊟ Yellow
- ◺ Pale Yellow

1 Square = 1 Stitch

33

This old-fashioned wooden Santa is destined to be carefully unwrapped each Christmas and hung in a traditional place of honor in your home. Children especially will look forward each year to seeing the kindly figure greeting them from a window or doorway as they come home from school or play.

If you're more comfortable working with craft materials other than wood, use your imagination to adapt the design to other techniques and materials. To help you, we've included some suggestions for using fabric paints, appliqué, and embroidery to turn this Santa into a soft figure or tree ornament.

Our St. Nicholas is 29½ inches tall.

MATERIALS

18x36-inch piece of ¼-inch-thick plywood
Sandpaper, wood filler
Gesso
Acrylic paints in jars (see photograph for colors)
Black India ink
Paintbrushes
Varnish, polyurethane, or clear acrylic sealer (optional)
Graph paper, carbon paper
Sawtooth picture hanger

INSTRUCTIONS

Enlarge the pattern, *right*, onto several sheets of graph paper taped together. Using carbon paper, transfer just the outline of the design to wood.

Cut out the figure along the traced outline using a jigsaw.

Fill any holes in the plywood edges with wood filler; let dry. Sand the edges and surface of the wood until smooth.

Prepare the wood for painting by coating the entire figure with gesso diluted with an equal amount of water. When dry, sand lightly with fine sandpaper until the surface and edges are perfectly smooth. Wipe the wood with a damp cloth to remove any dust. Add a second coat of gesso, if desired, then sand again when the gesso is completely dry.

Using carbon paper, transfer the rest of the design lines onto the wood.

Paint the design with acrylics, referring to the photograph for colors. Use a fine-tip brush to paint the edges of large areas, then fill in with a larger brush. Paint detailed areas last. (Always let paint dry thoroughly before painting adjacent areas.)

When the paint is dry, add black detail lines with India ink and a fine-tipped brush, or use a permanent fine-point marking pen. Let dry.

Acrylic paint dries to a permanent matte finish, so you need not coat the wood after it is painted. But for a shinier, more durable finish, varnish the figure, or coat it with polyurethane or clear acrylic sealer.

(Before applying any finish, check the compatibility of the paint and finish on a piece of scrap wood. If you use a marking pen for design details, draw some lines with the marker on scrap wood, then varnish over the lines to be sure the marker ink does not run.)

To varnish the wood, begin applying at the center and work toward the edges. Begin new strokes from the dry areas and work toward areas where the finish has been applied.

When the figure is dry, attach a sawtooth picture hanger to the back and hang as a window, door, or wall decoration.

- **Adapting the design:** If you prefer to work with fabric, you can make the St. Nicholas as a fabric figure to hang on the wall or to prop by the fireplace or a child's bed.

Cut the figure from muslin, allowing an extra 4-inch margin of fabric all around the design. Appliqué the clothing and add facial details with fabric paints, fine-tip markers, or simple embroidery stitches.

Mount the finished design on a piece of foam-core board cut to size and padded with quilt batting. Wrap the raw edges of the muslin to the back of the board and tape them into place.

Or, enlarge the pattern to tree ornament size (using a scale of 1 square equals ½ inch) and make a treeful of painted and embroidered Santas following the techniques used for the treetop angel on pages 18-21.

1 Square = 2 Inches

What better way is there to get into the party spirit of Christmas than with a festive table? To help you, we've gathered our loveliest linens, a whimsical centerpiece, and some elegant dish- ware for you to make now and enjoy for many Christmases to come.

Instructions for these four crocheted metallic edgings and the bell design on the doily begin on the next page.

The silver and gold crocheted edgings shown on pages 36-37 make dazzling holiday place mats, napkins, doilies, even curtains or garment trims. The bell motif shown on the round doily is crocheted, then tacked to linen. All of the other designs are crocheted directly onto the fabric.

Before you begin, sew a narrow rolled hem in the fabric. Then practice the crochet stitches on scrap fabric so you're sure they are uniform. When you work the edgings, you should have the same number of stitches on each edge of the fabric.

Crochet abbreviations are on page 73.

Crocheted Bell Edging

MATERIALS
One 175-yard ball of ecru Coats and Clark Knit-Cro-Sheen and size 7 steel crochet hook

Or H. Sherley No. 22 Starbright gold metallic thread and size B aluminum crochet hook

15½x20½ inches of ecru linen for a place mat, or 12½-inch-diameter circle of linen for doily

INSTRUCTIONS
This edging is worked in gold metallic thread on the round doily and in ecru thread on the panels hanging in the window.

Gauge: 1 repeat = 1¾ inches.
Ch 4. *Row 1:* 2 dc in 4th ch from hook, *ch 3, 3 dc in same ch*—shell made; ch 5, turn.

Row 2: In ch-3 sp of shell work *3 dc, ch 3, 3 dc*—shell over shell made; ch 3, turn.

Row 3: Shell over shell, *do not turn;* work 8 dc in ch-5 sp of turning lp bet 2 rows below; ch 3, turn.

Row 4: Dc in first dc and each dc across—9 dc in row, counting turning ch as dc; ch 3, turn.

Row 5: Dc in first dc and each dc across and in top of turning ch—10 dc in row, counting turning ch as dc; ch 2, turn.

Row 6: Sk first dc, hdc in next dc, dc in next 2 dc, trc in next dc, *ch 5, sl st in 5th ch from hook* —picot made; trc in next dc, dc in next 2 dc, hdc in next dc and top of turning ch, ch 7, work shell over shell; ch 3, turn.

Row 7: Shell over shell; ch 5, turn.

Row 8: Shell over shell; ch 3, turn.

Rows 9-10: Rep Rows 3-4.

Row 11: Rep Row 5, *do not turn* after ch-2 at end of row; join bell units with a sl st into 3rd ch of ch-7; ch 1, turn; sl st into each of next 2 ch and first dc; ch 2, hdc in next dc, dc in next 2 dc, trc in next dc, ch 5, sl st in 5th ch from hook—picot, trc in next st, dc in next 2 dc, hdc in next dc and top of turning ch, ch 7, shell over shell; ch 3, turn.

Rep Rows 7-11 to reach the desired length.

Tack the finished edging to hemmed linen.

To join work into a circle, end with Row 11; ch 4 instead of ch 7, sl st into top of ch-2 of next bell, ch 1, sl st back into next 2 ch, ch 5, 3 dc in ch-3 sp of shell, ch 1, sl st into bottom of next bell, ch 1, 3 dc in same ch-3 sp; ch 3, turn and sl st into top of first dc. Fasten off. Tack to hemmed edge of linen.

Gold Crocheted Edging

MATERIALS
One 20-gram ball of Phildar Sunset Gold metallic thread

12x12 inches of linen (or fabric sufficient for your project; adjust thread quantities accordingly)

Size 9 steel crochet hook

INSTRUCTIONS
This edging is shown at the far left in the photograph on pages 36-37.

Rnd 1: Attach thread to any corner of the linen, 3 sc in same corner, sc closely around, making 3 sc in each corner, making sure there are the same number of sts on each side of the fabric square. Sl st in first sc.

Rnd 2: In same place as sl st make sc and half dc, 3 dc in next sc, make half dc and sc in next sc, sc in next 7 sc, * half dc in next sc, dc in next 3 sc, half dc in next sc (scallop), sc in next 8 sc. Rep from * around, making sc and half dc in the first sc on each 3-sc grp at corners, 3 dc in the center sc and half dc and sc in the 3rd sc of each 3-sc grp at corners. Join sl st to first sc.

Rnd 3: Sl st in next half dc, ch 8, dc in 5th ch from hook (dc in next dc on scallop, ch 5, dc in last dc) 2 times; dc in next half dc of scallop, * ch 5, sk 4 sc, sc in next sc, ch 5, (dc in next dc on scallop, ch 5, dc in last dc) 3 times; dc in next half dc of scallop. Rep from * around. In corners make (dc in next dc on scallop, ch 5, dc in last dc) 3 times, dc in next half dc, ending with ch 5, sk 4 sc, sc in next sc, ch 5. Join ch-5 with sl st in first dc of rnd. Break off.

Ecru and Silver Crocheted Edging

MATERIALS
One 100-yard ball of Coats and Clark Knit-Cro-Sheen, No. 1S white and silver thread
16x16 inches of ecru linen (or fabric sufficient for your project; adjust thread quantities)
Size 8 steel crochet hook

INSTRUCTIONS
This edging is shown second from the left in the photograph.

Rnd 1: Attach thread to any corner of linen, sc closely all around, making 3 sc in each corner, sl st in first sc.

Rnd 2: Sl st in next 3 sc, sc in same sc, ch 5, sk 2 sc, sc in next sc. * ch 5, sk 3 sc, dc in next sc, ch 5, dc in last dc (picot), dc in same sc as the dc preceding the picot was made, ch 5, sk 3 sc, sc in next sc, ch 5, sk 2 sc, sc in next sc. Rep from * around, making sc, ch 5, and sc in center sc of each corner and ending with ch 5, sl st in first sc.

Rnd 3: Sl st in next 2 ch, sc in same lp, * ch 5, dc in next dc, (ch 5, dc in next dc) 3 times (3 picots made); sk next picot, dc in next dc, ch 5, sk next ch-5, sc in next ch-5 lp. Rep from * around. In corner make dc in next sc, (ch 5, dc in last dc) 4 times, sk next sp, dc in next sc, ch 5. Join ch-5 with sl st in first sc of rnd. Break off.

Ecru and Gold Crocheted Edging

MATERIALS
One 100-yard ball of Coats and Clark Knit-Cro-Sheen, No. 61G white and silver
16x16 inches of ecru linen (or sufficient fabric for your project; adjust thread quantities accordingly)
Size 8 steel crochet hook

INSTRUCTIONS
This edging is shown second from the right in the photograph on pages 36-37.

Rnd 1: Attach thread to one corner of linen, 3 sc in same place, make sc all around outer edges (12 sc to 1 in.), having 3 sc in each corner. Sl st in first sc.

Rnd 2: Sl st in next sc, ch 8, dc in same place as sl st, * ch 5, sk 3 sc, sc in next sc, ch 3, sk 1 sc, sc in next sc, ch 5, sk 3 sc, in next sc make dc, ch 3 and dc. Rep from * around, making dc, ch 5 and dc in center sc of each corner. Join with sl st to 3rd ch of ch-8.

Rnd 3: Sl st in next sp, ch 9, dc in 6th ch from hook, (dc in same sp, ch 5, dc in top of last dc made) 3 times; dc in same sp, * ch 5, sk next sp, sc in next lp, ch 5, sk next sp, in next sp make (dc, ch 5, dc in top of last dc made) 3 times and dc. Rep from * to corner, in corner sp make (dc, ch 5, dc in top of last dc made) 4 times and dc. Work other 3 sides to correspond. Join and break off.

Silver and Gold Lace Edging

MATERIALS
One 20-gram ball each of Phildar Sunset Gold and Sunset Silver metallic thread
12x12 inches of white linen (or fabric sufficient for your project; adjust thread quantities accordingly)
Size 9 steel crochet hook

INSTRUCTIONS
This edging is shown on the place mat at the far right in the photograph.

Rnd 1: Attach silver to corner of linen and sc closely around (24 sc to 1 inch), making 3 sc in each corner. Join with sl st to first sc. Break off.

Rnd 2: Attach gold to first sc, sc in same place, ch 4, sk 1 sc, sc in next sc, * ch 6, sk 4 sc, trc in next sc, ch 5, dc in last trc made, trc in same sc as last trc, ch 6, sk 4 sc. Sc in next sc, ch 4, sk 2 sc, sc in next sc. Rep from * across to within 4 sc of corner 3-sc grp, ending with ch-6. Sk 4 sc, sc in next sc, ch 4, sk 1 sc, sc in next sc. Work other sides and corners the same way. Join with sl st to first sc.

Rnd 3: Sl st in next lp, ch 7, in same lp make (double treble [dtr], ch 2) 4 times; * sk next sp, in next lp make (dtr, ch 2) 5 times; sk next sp, tr tr (triple treble) in next lp, ch 2. Rep from * across to next corner lp, ending with ch 2, in corner lp make (dtr, ch 2) 5 times. Work other sides and corners in the same way. Join last ch-2 with sl st to 5th ch of ch-7. Break off.

Rnd 4: Attach silver thread to first sp, sc in same place, * (ch 3, sc) 3 times; ch 5, sc in next sp, ch 5, sc in next sp, (ch 3, sc) 2 times. Rep from * around. Join and break off.

Protecting your lace
If you decide to put away your lace-edged place mats or doilies between holidays, take special care to store them properly so they won't be damaged during the year by dampness, yellowing, or fold marks that may weaken the threads.

First, find a box that is large enough to hold the unfolded place mats flat. Layer the place mats or doiles in the box with sheets of acid-free tissue paper in between. Then store the box in a cool, dry, dark place until the next holiday season.

Christmas is a season of elegance, a time to bring out your prettiest treasures to make every room in your house festive and inviting. And what could be more elegant than these cross-stitched place mats and napkins with their traditional rose and holly motifs? They're sure to be a favorite at any holiday celebration —whether it's a casual cookie exchange or your fanciest Christmas party.

MATERIALS

15x18 inches of ecru hardanger cloth for each place mat; 17½x17½ inches for each napkin

Embroidery floss in colors listed in color key, *below right*

Colored pencils, graph paper

Embroidery hoop

Small tapestry needle

Ecru thread

INSTRUCTIONS

The finished place mats are 12½x16 inches; to make larger mats, adjust materials and directions accordingly. Napkins measure 15½ inches square.

To create master patterns, tape sheets of graph paper together until they measure at least 23 inches square for the napkin, and at least 19x23 inches for the place mat. Use colored pencils to transfer the diagram, *right,* to the graph paper.

To transfer the design, begin in the corner and work toward the center, transferring the design from the chart. Complete the border by flopping the diagram and matching sides.

On the place mats, the outer border should be 27 scallops wide and 20 scallops deep, not including corner scallops. Each

side of the napkins has 26 scallops, not including corners.

Before you begin to stitch, preshrink and press the fabric. If you wish, you can mount the fabric in a frame, leaving both hands free for stitching.

Use three strands of floss for embroidery; work each stitch over two threads of fabric. Always work the cross-stitches in the same direction.

To begin, use a waste knot to anchor the thread end in the hardanger. Following the master pattern and the color key, *below,* make the first stitch 1½ inches from the edge and in the middle of one side of the fabric. Work the border design all the way around. When you finish a length of floss, clip off the beginning knot and weave the loose ends under the stitches.

On the place mats and napkins, cross-stitch the border motifs first. Then, on the place mats, work the rose and holly

design, following the diagram and counting threads carefully.

When you have finished the stitching, straighten the edges of the fabric for hemming by removing a thread 1 inch from the edge of the embroidery. Cut the fabric along the resulting channel to create a perfectly straight edge. Fold under ¼ inch along the raw edges of the hardanger, then turn under again for the hem. Baste and stitch.

Press the unembroidered portion of the place mats and napkins well, using spray starch if necessary. To press the embroidery, dampen and press gently on the wrong side of the fabric.

If you wish, you can adapt the rose and holly motif and borders to other Christmas projects, such as a tablecloth, guest towel, apron, or tree skirt. To be sure you are pleased with the design, first make a master pattern (using colored pencils) on graph paper.

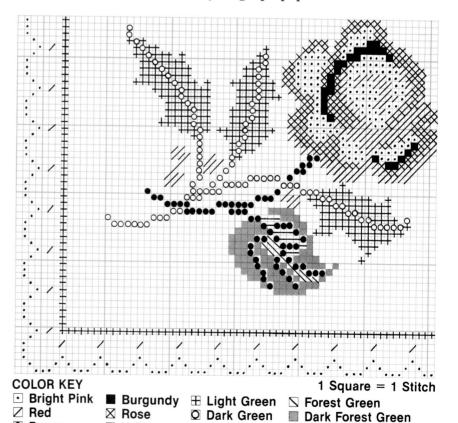

COLOR KEY   1 Square = 1 Stitch

⊡ Bright Pink	■ Burgundy	⊞ Light Green	◺ Forest Green
⧄ Red	☒ Rose	◎ Dark Green	▨ Dark Forest Green
● Brown	⊟ Yellow		

With the old-fashioned elegance of antique lace, this crocheted tablecloth makes a lovely addition to your holiday table. The rings of pineapple medallions, a traditional symbol of hospitality, create a complementary backdrop for any table setting.

42

MATERIALS
Thirteen 400-yard balls of American Thread Company "Giant" thread, size 9 steel crochet hook
Or, 20 balls of Coats and Clark Knit-Cro-Sheen, size 7 hook

INSTRUCTIONS
The finished tablecloth is 72 inches in diameter.

For crochet abbreviations, see page 73.

Beg at center, ch 8, join with sl st to form ring.

Rnd 1: Ch 1, sc in ring, (ch 9, sc in ring) 7 times; ch 5, dtr in first sc to form last lp—8 lps.

Rnd 2: Ch 1, sc in lp just formed, ch 7, (sc in next lp, ch 7) 7 times; sl st in first sc.

Rnd 3: Ch 3, dc in joining— starting cl (cluster) made, * ch 3, sc in next lp, ch 3, 2 dc in next sc; *holding last lp of each dc on hook, thread over and draw through all lps on hook—cl made.* Rep from * around, end with ch 3, join with sl st in dc.

Note: On each following rnd, repeat from * around, end as given and then join as in Rnd 3.

Rnd 4: 2 dc cl in tip of first cl, * ch 4, *(sc, ch 9, sc) in next sc—lp inc made;* ch 4, cl in tip of next cl, end ch 4.

Rnd 5: * Cl over cl, ch 7, sc in next lp, ch 7.

Rnd 6: * Cl over cl, ch 3, sc in next lp, ch 3, cl in next sc, ch 3, sc in next lp, ch 3.

Rnd 7: * Cl over cl, ch 4, sc in next sc, ch 4.

Rnd 8: * Cl over cl, ch 9.

Rnd 9: * Cl over cl, ch 4, sc in next lp, ch 4.

Rnd 10: Work as for Rnd 4, making ch 5 instead of ch 4.

Rnds 11-15: Rep Rnds 5-9.

Rnd 16: * Cl over cl, ch 5, sc over sc, ch 5.

Rnd 17: * In tip of cl make (2 dc cl, ch 3, 2 dc cl)—cl shell over cluster, ch 8, cl over cl, ch 8.

Rnd 18: * Cl over cl, ch 2, cl in next sp, ch 2, (cl over cl, ch 3, sc in next lp, ch 3) twice.

Rnd 19: * Cl over cl, ch 2, *in tip of next cl make (cl, ch 5, cl)—pineapple lp over cl made;* ch 2, (cl over cl, ch 3, sc over sc, ch 3) twice.

Rnd 20: * Cl over cl, ch 2, 11 dc in lp (pineapple base), ch 2, (cl over cl, ch 2) twice.

Rnd 21: * Cl over cl, (ch 1, dc in next dc) 11 times; ch 1, (cl over cl, ch 1) twice.

Rnd 22: Cl over cl, * ch 2, sk next sp, across pineapple make sc in first sp, (ch 3, sc in next sp) 9 times; ch 2, (cl over cl) 3 times; end (cl over cl) twice.

Rnd 23: Cl over cl, * ch 3, (sc in next lp, ch 3) 8 times; sc in last lp, ch 3, (cl over cl) 3 times; end (cl over cl) twice.

Rnd 24: * Cl over cl, ch 4, (sc in next lp, ch 3) 7 times; sc in last pineapple lp, ch 4, cl over cl, sk next cl.

Note: Hereafter, when working across pineapples, there will be 1 lp less on each rnd.

Rnd 25: Cl over cl, * ch 4, work across lps as before in this and following rnds, ch 4, (cl over

cl) twice; end cl over cl.

Rnd 26: * Cl over cl, ch 5, work across lps, ch 5, cl over cl, ch 2.

Rnd 27: * Cl over cl, ch 5, work across lps, ch 5, cl over cl, ch 1, cl in next sp, ch 1.

Rnd 28: * Cl over cl, ch 5, work across lps, ch 5, cl over cl, ch 3, ch 6 pineapple stem in next cl, ch 3.

Rnd 29: * Cl over cl, ch 5, work across lps, ch 5, cl over cl, ch 2, 12 dc in pineapple lp, ch 2.

Rnd 30: * Cl over cl, ch 5, work across lps, ch 5, cl over cl, (ch 1, dc in next dc) 12 times; ch 1.

Rnd 31: * Cl over cluster, ch 4, sc in pineapple lp, ch 4, cl over cl, ch 3, sk next sp, (sc in next sp, ch 3) 11 times.

Rnds 32, 33: * (Cl over cl) twice; ch 4, work across the lps, ch 4.

Rnd 34: * Cl over cl, ch 2, cl over cl, ch 5, work across the lps, ch 5.

Rnd 35: * Cl over cl, ch 2, cl in next sp, ch 2, cl over cl, ch 5, work across lps, ch 5.

Rnd 36: * (Cl over cl, ch 5) twice; cl over cl, ch 5, work across lps, ch 5.

Rnd 37: * (Cl over cl, ch 2, sc in next lp, ch 2) twice; cl over cl, ch 5, work across lps, ch 5.

Rnd 38: * (Cl over cl, ch 3, inc lp in next sc, ch 3) twice; cl over cl, ch 5, work across lps, ch 5.

Rnd 39: * (Cl over cl, ch 7, sc in inc lp, ch 7) twice; cl over cl, ch 5, work across lps, ch 5.

Rnd 40: * (Cl over cl, ch 3, sc in next lp, ch 3, cl in next sc, ch 3, sc in next lp, ch 3) twice; cl over cl, ch 5, work across the lp, ch 5.

Rnd 41: * (Cl over cl, ch 5, sc over sc, ch 5) 4 times; cl over cl, ch 4, sc in pineapple lp, ch 4.

Rnd 42: * (Cl over cl, (ch 10, cl over cl) 4 times.

Rnd 43: * (Cl over cl, ch 4, sc in the next lp, ch 4) 4 times; cl over cl.

Rnd 44: * (Cl over cl, ch 5, sc over sc, ch 5) twice; cl shell over cl, (ch 5, sc over sc, ch 5, cl over cl) twice.

Rnd 45: * (Cl over cl, ch 9) twice; cl over cl, ch 2, cl in next sp, ch 2 (cl over cl, ch 9) twice; cl over cl, ch 2.

Rnd 46: * (Cl over cl, ch 3, sc in next lp, ch 3) twice; (cl over cl, ch 3) twice; (cl over cl, ch 3, sc in next lp, ch 3) twice; cl over cl, ch 3, cl in next sp, ch 3.

Rnd 47: * (Cl over cl, ch 3, sc over sc, ch 3) twice; cl over cl, ch 2, ch 6 pineapple lp over cl, ch 2.

Rnd 48: * (Cl over cl, ch 3) 3 times; 12 dc in pineapple lp, ch 3. *Rnd 49:* * (Cl over cl, ch 1) 3 times; (dc in next dc, ch 1) 12 times. Fasten off. Join thread to third cl on rnd.

Rnds 50-57: Work as for Rnds 22-29, making 10 pineapple lps on Rnd 50, 9 pineapple lps on Rnd 51, 8 pineapple lps on Rnd 52 and 13 dc in pineapple stem lp on Rnd 57 for pineapples.

Rnd 58: * Cl over cl, ch 5, work across lps, ch 5, cl over cl, (ch 1, dc in next dc) 13 times; ch 1. Fasten off. Join thread to second cluster on rnd.

Rnd 59: * Cl over cl, ch 3, sk next sp, (sc in next sp, ch 3) 12 times; cl over cl, ch 5, make pineapple lp, ch 5.

Rnd 60: * Cl over cl, ch 3, work across lps, ch 3, cl over cl, ch 5, sc in pineapple lp, ch 5.

Rnds 61, 62: Rep Rnd 25.

Rnds 63-67: Work as for Rnds 26-29 and Rnd 58, making ch 7 pineapple lps on Rnd 65, 14 dc in pineapple lp on Rnd 66 and 14 dc for pineapples on Rnd 67. Don't fasten off at end of Rnd 67. (*Note:* Hereafter, make ch 4 lps on new pineapples.)

Rnd 68: * Cl over cl, ch 5, work across lps, ch 5, cl over cl, ch 3, sk next sp, (sc in next sp, ch 4) 12 times; sc in next sp, ch 3.

Rnd 69: * Cl over cl, ch 5, work across lps, ch 5. Fasten off. Join thread to next cl.

Rnd 70: Work as for Rnd 60, making ch-5 sps before and after pineapple lps.

Note: Hereafter, make ch-6 sps before and after all pineapple lps.

Rnds 71-72: Repeat Rnd 25.

Rnds 73-77: Work as for Rnds 26-29 and Rnd 58, making ch-9 pineapple lps on Rnd 75, 15 dc in pineapple lp on Rnd 76 and 15 dc for pineapples on Rnd 77. Fasten off at end of Rnd 77. Join thread to next cl.

Continued

43

Rnd 78: * Cl over cl, ch 3, sk next sp, (sc in next sp, ch 4) 13 times; sc in next sp, ch 3, cl over cl, ch 6, sc in pineapple lp, ch 6.

Rnd 79: * Cl over cl, ch 3, work across lps, ch 3, cl over cl, ch 6, make pineapple lp, ch 6.

Rnd 80: * Cl over cl, ch 4, work across lps, ch 4, cl over cl, ch 6, sc in pineapple lp, ch 6. Fasten off. Join thread to next cl. (*Note:* Where rnds are worked as for previous rnds, continue to ch 6 before and after pineapple lps.)

Rnds 81-89: Work as for Rnds 32-40, making 2 pineapple lps on Rnd 89. Fasten off at end of Rnd 89. Join thread to last cl made.

Rnd 90: * Cl over cl, ch 6, work across lp, ch 6, (cl over cl, ch 4, sc over sc, ch 4) 4 times.

Rnd 91: * Cl over cl, ch 6, sc in pineapple lp, ch 6, (cl over cl, ch 10) 4 times.

Rnd 92: Cl over cl, * (cl over cl, ch 4, sc in next lp, ch 4) twice, make 2 cl in next cl, (ch 4, sc in next lp, ch 4, cl over cl) twice; end ch 4.

Rnd 93: * Cl over cl, (cl over cl, ch 5, sc over sc, ch 5) twice; cl over cl, ch 2, (cl over cl, ch 5, sc over sc, ch 5) twice.

Rnd 94: * Cl over cl, ch 1, (cl over cl, ch 10) twice; cl over cl, ch 1, cl in next sp, ch 1, (cl over cl, ch 10) twice.

Rnd 95: * Cl over cl, ch 2, (cl over cl, ch 4, sc in next lp, ch 4) twice; (cl over cl, ch 2) twice; (cl over cl, ch 4, sc in next lp, ch 4) twice.

Rnd 96: * Cl over cl, ch 3, (cl over cl, ch 5, sc over sc, ch 5) twice; (cl over cl, ch 3) twice; (cl over cl, ch 5, sc over sc, ch 5) twice.

Rnd 97: * Cl over cl, ch 8.

Rnd 98: * Cl over cl, ch 3, sc in next lp, ch 3.

Rnd 99: * Cl over cl, ch 4, inc lp in next sc, ch 4, (cl over cl, ch 4, sc over sc, ch 4) 6 times.

Rnd 100: * Cl over cl, ch 6, sc in next inc lp, ch 6, (cl over cl, ch 8) 6 times.

Rnd 101: * Cl over cl, ch 3, sc in next lp, ch 3, cl in next sc, ch 3, sc in next lp, ch 3, (cl over cl, ch 3, sc in next lp, ch 3) 6 times.

Rnd 102: * Cl over cl, ch 4, sc over sc, ch 4.

Rnds 103-107: Repeat Rnds 97, 98, 102, 97, and 98.

Rnd 108: (Cl over cl, ch 4, sc over sc, ch 4) 4 times; * cl over cl, ch 4, sc over sc, ch 1, ch 9 pineapple lp in next cl, ch 1, sc over sc, ch 4, (cl over cl, ch 4, sc over sc, ch 4) 6 times; end ch 4. Fasten off. Join thread to fourth cl on rnd.

Rnd 109: * Cl over cl, ch 8, cl over cl, ch 1, 18 tr in next pineapple lp, ch 1, sk next sc, (cl over cl, ch 8) 5 times.

Rnd 110: * Cl over cl, ch 4, sc in next lp, (ch 1, tr in next tr) 18 times; ch 1, sc in next lp, ch 4, (cl over cl, ch 3, sc in next lp, ch 3) 4 times.

Rnd 111: * Cl over cl, ch 4, sk next tr, sc in next sp, (ch 5, sc in next sp) 16 times; ch 4, (cl over cl, ch 4, sc over sc, ch 4) twice; cl shell over cl, ch 4, sc over sc, ch 4, cl over cl, ch 4, sc over sc, ch 4.

(*Note:* Hereafter, make ch-5 lps on pineapples.)

Rnd 112: * Cl over cl, ch 4, work across lps, ch 4, (cl over cl, ch 7) 5 times.

Rnd 113: * Cl over cl, ch 4, work across lps, ch 4, (cl over cl, ch 3, sc in next lp, ch 3) 5 times.

Rnd 114: * Cl over cl, ch 4, work across lps, ch 4, (cl over cl, ch 4, sc over sc, ch 4) 5 times.

Rnd 115: * Cl over cl, ch 4, work across lps, ch 4, (cl over cl, ch 8) 5 times.

Rnd 116: Repeat Rnd 113.

Rnd 117: * Cl over cl, ch 5, work across lps, ch 5, (cl over cl, ch 4, sc over sc, ch 4) 5 times.

Rnd 118: * Cl over cl, ch 5, work across lps, ch 5, (cl over cl, ch 9) 5 times.

Rnd 119: * Cl over cl, ch 5, work across lps, ch 5, (cl over cl, ch 4, sc in next lp, ch 4) 5 times.

Rnd 120: * Cl over cl, ch 5, work across lps, ch 5, (cl over cl, ch 4, sc over sc, ch 4) twice; cl over cl, ch 4, inc lp in next sc, ch 4, (cl over cl, ch 4, sc over sc, ch 4) twice.

Rnd 121: * Cl over cl, ch 5, work across lps, ch 5, (cl over cl, ch 10) 3 times; sc in next inc lp, ch 10, (cl over cl, ch 10) twice.

Rnd 122: * Cl over cl, ch 5, work across lps, ch 5, (cl over cl, ch 4, sc in next lp, ch 4) 3 times; cl in next sc, ch 4, sc in next lp, ch 4, (cl over cl, ch 4, sc in next lp, ch 4) twice.

Rnd 123: * Cl over cl, ch 5, work across lps, ch 5, (cl over cl, ch 5, sc over sc, ch 5) 3 times; cl shell over cl, ch 5, sc over sc, ch 5, (cl over cl, ch 5, sc over sc, ch 5) twice.

Rnd 124: * Cl over cl, ch 5, work across lps, ch 5, (cl over cl, ch 12) 3 times; cl over cl, ch 5, (cl over cl, ch 12) 3 times.

Rnd 125: * Cl over cl, ch 5, work across lps, ch 5, (cl over cl, ch 5, sc in next lp, ch 5) 3 times; cl over cl, ch 4, sc in next lp, ch 4, (cl over cl, ch 5, sc in next lp, ch 5) 3 times.

Rnd 126: * Cl over cl, ch 6, work across lps, ch 6, (cl over cl, ch 6, sc over sc, ch 6) 7 times.

Rnd 127: * Cl over cl, ch 6, sc in pineapple lp, ch 6, (cl over cl, ch 13) 7 times.

Rnd 128: * (Cl over cl) twice; ch 6, sc in next lp, ch 6, (cl over cl, ch 6, sc in next lp, ch 6) 6 times.

Rnd 129: * Cl over cl, ch 3, cl over cl, (ch 5, sc over sc, ch 5, cl shell over cl) 6 times; ch 5, sc over sc, ch 5. Fasten off. Press.

Embellished with a traditional poinsettia motif, these hand-painted dishes will lend a festive touch to your holiday meals and parties for years to come.

MATERIALS

Greenware pitcher and platter (available from ceramics studios)
Duncan's underglaze in red, orange, green, and translucent jade green
Duncan's ultraclear glaze
Small ceramics sponge
Small paintbrush for details
Larger paintbrush for overall design
Graph paper, carbon paper

INSTRUCTIONS

The platter we used is approximately 11x17 inches, and the pitcher is about 3 inches in diameter and 10½ inches tall. If the ceramic pieces available to you come in different sizes or shapes, adapt the designs to fit.

Greenware is extremely fragile, so handle it with care. Use a damp ceramics sponge to clean each piece and smooth rough edges and seams. Wipe with a damp towel to remove clay dust.

After cleaning pieces, have them fired to bisque at a ceramics shop. The pieces will then be stronger and easier to handle.

Enlarge the pattern, *below right,* to the appropriate size for your pieces. The scale shown is for the platter design; resize the pattern to fit the pitcher. Transfer the design onto each piece using pencil and carbon paper.

Apply underglaze, following the manufacturer's directions. Paint pine needles and veins in jade green using a small brush. Paint remaining design with larger brush, referring to photograph for colors.

Let first coat dry thoroughly. Apply two more coats, letting each dry. Layer coats carefully so edges are crisp, not blurry.

When the underglaze is completely dry, apply a clear glaze: Thin the glaze with water to a creamy consistency and pat a thin coat over each bisque piece with a clean, damp sponge. Let the first coat dry thoroughly, then apply two more coats.

(When the pieces are properly glazed, the poinsettia motif will barely show through. This will change as the glaze dries.)

Let the pieces dry thoroughly, then fire them a final time at a ceramics shop.

1 Square = 1 Inch

Capture the rollicking spirit of a country sleigh ride with this miniature tole-painted cutter. Fill it with greenery and fruits for a Christmas feast or with gaily wrapped favors and candies for a children's party. Either way, this 14-inch-long sleigh makes a lively focal point for your holiday table.

The basic construction is simple; just cut the pieces from plywood, then nail and glue them together. Take a little extra time, though, to make sure the beveled edges of *the floor, seat, and back pieces turn out just right. Then spruce up the sides with a pretty bouquet.*

MATERIALS
⅜-inch-thick plywood
Small finishing nails
Wood glue
Sandpaper
Carbon paper
Wood sealer
Acrylic paints
Decorative painting equipment
Satin finish varnish

INSTRUCTIONS
The finished sleigh is 14 inches long and 7 inches high.

Enlarge the patterns, *opposite,* for the sides, front, back, floor, and seat pieces. Transfer the patterns to plywood. (Or use cedar, instead, for a pleasant Christmas-scented sleigh.)

Cut the side pieces from plywood, then cut the remaining pieces with beveled edges as indicated on the diagram.

Bevel-cut the back of the sleigh at 100 degrees and the front at 120 degrees. Cut the bottom of the back at 80 degrees so that it fits flush with the floor end. Cut the bottom of the front piece on a 60-degree angle so it fits flush. Bevel the top of the back and the top of the front so that they slope down toward the outside.

Attach the seat to the back piece with glue and nails. (Drill nail holes for each nail before attaching.) Then glue and nail the back piece to the floor. Attach the front piece to the floor. See the dotted lines on the side pattern piece for positioning.

Before attaching the sides, lay them on the center assembly. Draw guidelines on the inside of one side piece to mark the position of the center assembly. Drill nail holes to fall within the center of center pieces.

Drill, glue, and nail one side piece to the center assembly. Then place the sleigh on its runners, pressing the unattached side in position so that both runners "ride" smoothly on the surface and the sleigh doesn't wobble. Similarly draw and drill the remaining side; secure in place.

Sand smooth all edges and surfaces; seal the exposed edges of the plywood. Give the sleigh two base coats, using white acrylic paint (sand between coats). Then paint the runners, edges of the sides, seat, front, and back gold. Paint the top surface of the seat black. Paint the remaining surfaces red.

Next, enlarge the floral pattern, *right,* and transfer it to the wood using graphite paper.

To paint the roses, use a fine-tipped brush to fill in the black circle at the top of each rose. With bright pink paint, make two or three strokes across the lower portion of each flower for highlights. Add gold and white dots to the black area.

Paint a base of black behind the roses before adding leaves. Paint leaves in dark and light greens, then add the black wispy stems. Outline the side pieces with thin black lines. Finish with two coats of satin-finish varnish.

Or, instead of painting the sleigh, finish it with stain and varnish or a wash of color from diluted fabric dye.

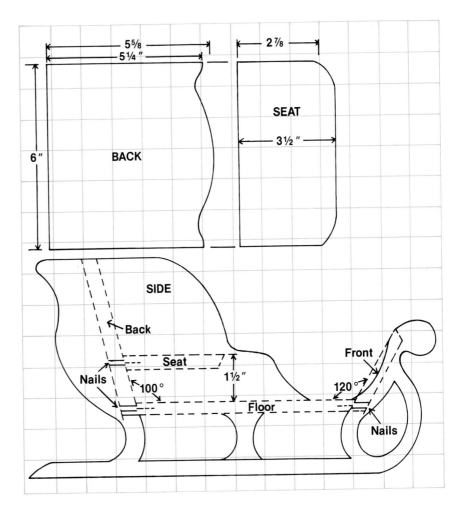

1 Square = 1 Inch

TREATS FOR THE YOUNG AT HEART

As "children" of all ages know, the best Christmas treats aren't always tucked beneath the tree! For example, a mantel or tabletop would be the ideal setting for this miniature, magical village, which is painted and embellished in the colors of your choice.

By following the simple instructions on the next few pages, you can also embroider a pair of pictures to prop beside a youngster's bed, stitch a toy-bedecked wreath to greet guests at the front door, or craft a trio of stockings that, when hung from the mantel, will melt the heart of Scrooge himself. For these and other projects, please turn the page.

49

What better way to charm your children at Christmastime than with the delightful village shown on pages 48-49! Complete with removable roofs, these one- and two-story buildings can be used as substitute stockings, gift boxes, centerpieces filled with candies and greenery or, of course, as an enchanting gift for children to play with all year long.

MATERIALS

⅜-inch plywood
Primer paint, acrylic paint in various colors, acrylic gloss medium, paintbrushes
Dollhouse wallpapers
¾-inch-wide dollhouse gingerbread trims (available at miniatures stores)
⅛-inch-thick balsa wood
White glue; 1-inch brads
Black felt-tip marker
Optional: tagboard, purchased dollhouse window and Toy Shop sign

INSTRUCTIONS

The buildings shown on pages 48-49 are constructed in three styles—a simple two-story (the Toy Shop), a cottage (the pink and white buildings), and a two-story Tudor. The orange building is the upper floor of the simple two-story design.

The two-story and Tudor houses are actually two boxes, with one set atop the other. The cottage is a single box trimmed to look like a two-story house.

• **Cutting the pieces:** Cut pieces from plywood according to the following directions.

• *Simple two-story house:* For *each* of the two stories, cut one 2¾x6¾-inch piece for the floor and two 4½x6¾-inch pieces for the front and back walls. For the first story, cut two 3½x4½-inch pieces for the end walls. For the second story, cut the end walls according to the measurements on the Toy Shop end wall pattern, *opposite.*

For roof pieces, cut a 4¼x8-inch rectangle and a 4x8-inch rectangle. Cut two roof supports along the cutting line for the Toy Shop (see pattern, *opposite*). If you wish, rout the exterior walls at ½-inch intervals.

• *Cottage:* Cut a 4¼x6¾-inch floor and two 6¾-inch-square pieces for the front and back walls. Cut two end walls according to the cottage end wall pattern, *opposite.* For roof pieces, cut a 4¾x8-inch and 4½x8-inch rectangle. Cut two roof supports (see pattern).

• *Two-story Tudor:* For the first story, cut a 4¾x9¾-inch floor, two 5¼x9¾-inch pieces for the front and back walls, and two 5¼x5½-inch end walls.

For the Tudor's second story, cut a 5¾x11¾-inch floor and two 4¼x11¾-inch pieces for the front and back walls. Cut two end walls according to the pattern, *opposite.* For the roof pieces, cut a 6¼x12½-inch and a 6x12½-inch rectangle. Cut two roof supports (see pattern).

From balsa wood, cut four dormer roofs and two dormer windows according to the patterns, *opposite.*

• **Assembling the buildings:** Glue and nail the front and back walls to the floor. Then attach the end walls. To assemble the roof, glue and nail the roof pieces together, tucking the narrower piece under the wider one. Sand the joints to fit. Sand off the slope of the lower roof into a vertical edge. Glue and nail the roof supports 1 inch in from the ends of the roof so they will fit inside the house walls.

To assemble the dormers on the roof of the Tudor, glue the dormer roofs together at the top, then glue the dormers to the roof along the valley edges. Glue the windows inside the dormers.

• **Painting and wallpapering:** Coat the building exteriors with primer paint. Let dry, then paint in the color of your choice. Wallpaper the interiors.

Paint the roof a solid color, or paint it gray and, using a black marker, draw in the roof patterning, *opposite.*

• **Adding doors and windows:** There are six different window designs to choose from. For patterns, see Windows 1, 2, and 3, the end wall of the Tudor, and the dormer window, *opposite.* The sixth window is a purchased octagonal frame, shown in the photograph on the end of the white cottage.

For smooth-sided buildings, pencil the appropriate window pattern on the building. Paint the window area yellow. Outline the frame, panes, and other details with black marker; add painted strips of ¼-inch-wide balsa wood, if desired.

To add windows and doors to routed buildings, paint them on tagboard, cut them out, and glue them to the exterior.

• *To create a door,* draw a rectangle from the bottom of the building to the height of the top of the windows. Paint, then add details with black marker and painted ¼-inch-wide strips of balsa wood.

Or, make a rounded door as shown on the pink cottage by following the pattern for Window 1 and extending the design to the bottom of the building. Paint and add details as explained for the windows.

• **Adding trims:** Glue lengths of gingerbread trim or ¼-inch-wide balsa wood strips along the eaves and walls of the buildings.

• **Finishing:** Coat the exterior of the completed buildings with acrylic gloss medium. If you wish, "age" the buildings by sponging paint at random on the exterior walls.

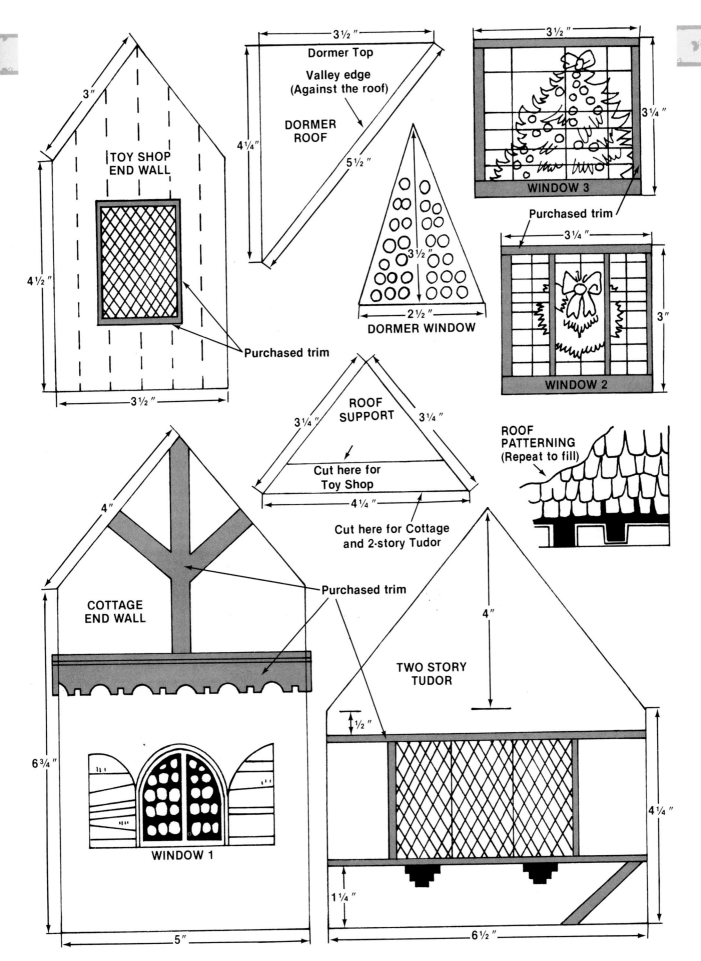

TOY SHOP
END WALL

Purchased trim

3"

4½"

3½"

Dormer Top

Valley edge
(Against the roof)

DORMER
ROOF

3½"

4¼"

5½"

DORMER WINDOW

3½"

2½"

WINDOW 3

3½"

3¼"

Purchased trim

WINDOW 2

3¼"

3"

ROOF
SUPPORT

3¼"

3¼"

Cut here for
Toy Shop

Cut here for Cottage
and 2-story Tudor

4¼"

ROOF
PATTERNING
(Repeat to fill)

COTTAGE
END WALL

4"

Purchased trim

6¾"

WINDOW 1

5"

TWO STORY
TUDOR

4"

½"

4¼"

1¼"

6½"

51

All a child's dreams come true in the ring of Victorian toys shown here and on the cover. Finish it as a fanciful wreath, or stitch it into a spectacular frame for a treasured photograph.

MATERIALS
26x26 inches of muslin
Brown pen, graph paper
Fabric paint, brushes
Embroidery floss in assorted colors, embroidery hoop
Beads; buttons; and scraps of fabric, ribbon, and lace

For framed wreath: Four 3½ x26-inch strips of fabric for border, three yards of velvet ribbon, quilt batting, purchased frame

For cover wreath: 26x26 inches of muslin for backing, quilt batting and foam core board cut to appropriate size, lace

INSTRUCTIONS

Enlarge pattern, *below,* onto graph paper, or have a photo-engraving shop enlarge it photographically. With pen, trace onto muslin. (*Note:* In lower left corner of the pattern are pine needles to work as background behind toys. If you do not wish to include this stitching, *do not trace these lines.*)

Referring to photographs, *opposite* and *on the cover,* and to instructions on page 19, paint the designs in desired colors.

Embellish the toys with a variety of embroidery stitches and colors. In the background, make French knots, or outline stitch pine needles in green. If desired, add decorative beads, buttons, appliqués, ribbons, and laces.

• *For framed wreath,* embroider ribbons in corners by tracing the bow, *below,* and transferring to muslin. Stitch. Using ½-inch seam margins, stitch fabric border strips to edges of wreath. Stitch ribbon over the seams.

Cut out the center of wreath, turn under raw edge, and trim with velvet ribbon. Cut a circular mat for the center, add a family photograph, stretch the fabric over a layer of quilt batting atop a board, and frame.

• *For cover wreath,* cut out center of wreath. Sandwich batting and foam core board between wreath front and muslin back; blindstitch. Add lace to edges.

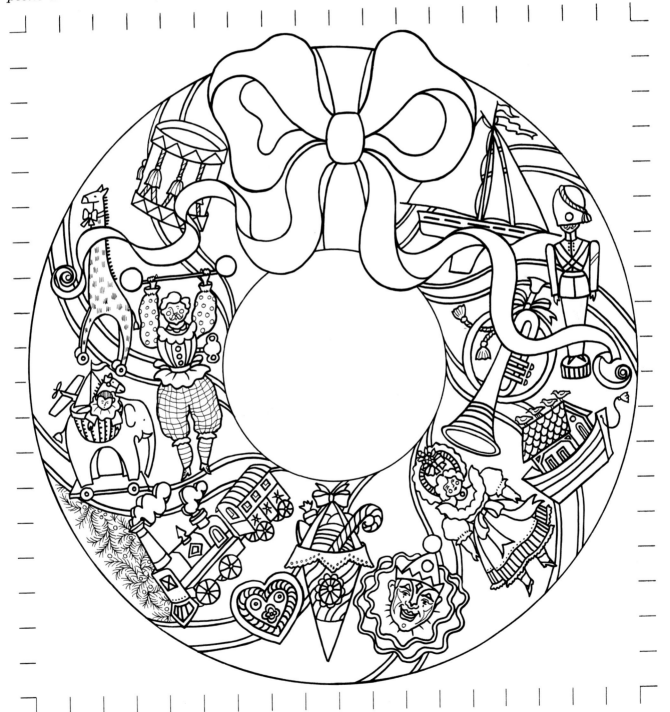

1 Square = 1 Inch

Yesteryear Stocking

Like a classic Victorian crazy quilt, this stocking glimmers with fanciful patterns and colors. There's even a patch on which to embroider the year of your child's birth, creating a personalized stocking to display with pride every year.

MATERIALS
1 yard of muslin
½ yard of polyester fleece
Butcher paper
Brown fine-point permanent marker
Green and burgundy fabric paints, small paintbrushes
Embroidery floss in rich colors and metallics
Embroidery hoop, needle
Assorted beads and decorative buttons, ecru thread
5⅝ yards of burgundy rattail cording, twisted into 1¾ yards

INSTRUCTIONS
Using hatch marks around the pattern as guides, draw a grid over the pattern, *right;* enlarge the pattern onto butcher paper. Then center the pattern under 15x20 inches of muslin and lightly trace the design with a fine-point marker.

To decorate the stocking as shown in the photograph, first paint most of the patches with light shades of green and burgundy. (For details on fabric painting, see page 19). Leave a few of the patches unpainted.

When the paint is completely dry, set the colors by pressing the stocking on the wrong side.

Embellish the stocking with touches of embroidery, referring to the photograph for color and stitch suggestions. Use a variety of metallic threads and colored floss to cover the brown design lines and fill in motifs.

Add beads and novelty buttons to the centers of the hearts, flowers, and butterfly wings, or just to add sparkle to a plain muslin patch. (For information on other fabric decorating techniques, see pages 18-21).

After decorating, cut out the stocking ¾ inch beyond the outline; cut a matching fleece interlining and muslin backing. Baste the fleece to the wrong side of the stocking front. Then, with right sides facing, sew the front and back together ¼ inch outside the outline. Leave the top open. Trim the seam and clip the curves.

To line the stocking, cut two pieces of muslin the same size as the stocking front. With the right sides facing, sew around the edge of the lining; leave the top open. Trim the seam; clip the curves.

With wrong sides facing, slip the lining over the stocking. Turn under ¼ inch on the top edges; blindstitch them together. Turn right side out.

Sew twisted yarn cord to the seams; add a hanging loop.

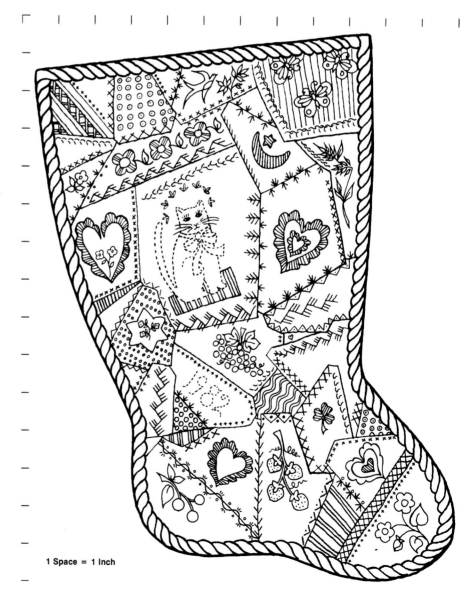

1 Space = 1 Inch

The carrot-nosed snowman grinning from this stocking will delight your children as much as the Christmas-morning goodies stuffed inside. With one simple needlepoint stitch and several cheery-colored yarns, the stocking creates a delightful 12x18-inch background for the dapper snowman.

MATERIALS

16x22 inches each of No. 10-count needlepoint canvas and quilted backing fabric
32-inch strands of 5-ply Persian yarn in the following amounts and colors:
10 dark red, 18 light red, 10 dark green, 20 light green, 10 dark blue, 25 light blue, 3 yellow, and 10 light orange
32-inch strands of 3-ply yarn in these amounts and colors:
50 white, 12 black, 4 yellow, 1 pink, 15 dark orange
Scrap of fabric for facing
½ yard of lining fabric
1½ yards of red cording
Needlepoint frame or stretcher bars, tapestry needle

INSTRUCTIONS

To minimize distortion of the canvas while you work, mount it on stretchers or a needlework frame. Begin stitching in the middle of the canvas (and in the center of the diagram, *right*). Use the mosaic stitch (see the diagram, *right*) and three plies of yarn throughout.

Work the stocking, following the color key, *right*. Leave 2 inches of unworked canvas all around the stitched design.

When you have finished the stitching, block the needlepoint by steam pressing with a warm iron on the wrong side. Trim excess canvas ½ inch beyond the edge of the needlepoint.

From quilted fabric, cut a back to match front. With right sides facing, sew the back to the front, stitching between the first and second rows of stitches on the needlepoint. Clip curves.

From a scrap of fabric, cut a 2-inch-wide facing strip that is long enough to go around the top of the stocking. Seam it along the short edges to make a continuous piece of fabric.

With the right sides together, match a long edge of the facing to the top edge of the stocking; stitch. Turn facing to the wrong side of the stocking.

On the lining fabric, trace the shape of the stocking. Add a ½-inch seam allowance, then cut a front and back. With right sides together, stitch, leaving the top open. Trim 1 inch from the top of the lining; fold under ½ inch along the edge and press.

With wrong sides together, slip the lining over the stocking. Blindstitch the folded edge of the lining to the facing. Turn the stocking right side out and tuck the lining inside.

Whipstitch purchased cording over the edge of the stocking. Add hanging loop to top.

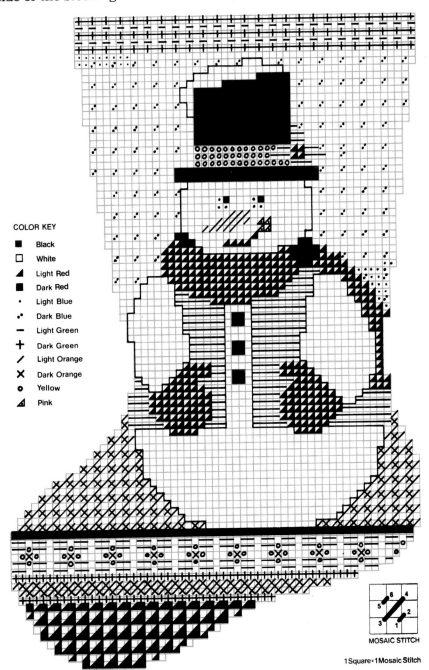

COLOR KEY

- ■ Black
- □ White
- ◪ Light Red
- ■ Dark Red
- · Light Blue
- • Dark Blue
- − Light Green
- + Dark Green
- ╱ Light Orange
- ✕ Dark Orange
- ○ Yellow
- ◪ Pink

MOSAIC STITCH

1 Square = 1 Mosaic Stitch

Just like a scene from a favorite fairy tale, this needlepoint Christmas stocking is sheer enchantment. Its colorful candy canes, glittering stars, and subtle shadings make this design as fanciful and inviting as the fuzzy cottontails on the trio of sleeping bunnies.

MATERIALS

18x26 inches of No. 12-count mono needlepoint canvas

One 40-yard skein *each* of Elsa Williams tapestry yarn (or a suitable substitute) in the following colors: N801 black, N805 off-white, N715 beige, N714 tan, N713 light brown, N712 brown, N424 light green, N423 medium green, N422 bright green, N112 red, N900 white, N501 dark navy

Two 40-yard skeins N531 navy Elsa Williams tapestry yarn (or a suitable substitute)

Small pieces of yellow yarn

Silver cloisonné thread

No. 18 tapestry needle

Needlepoint frame or artists' stretcher bars, masking tape

⅓ yard of navy velveteen backing fabric

½ yard of lining fabric

2 yards of twisted red yarn cording

INSTRUCTIONS

Before you begin stitching, bind the edges of the needlepoint canvas with masking tape to prevent them from raveling. Then, to minimize distortion, stretch the canvas on a frame or stretcher bars. Cut the yarn into 18- to 20-inch lengths. (Use a yarn caddy to keep strands sorted by color.)

Follow the general instructions on page 60 as you work.

Continued

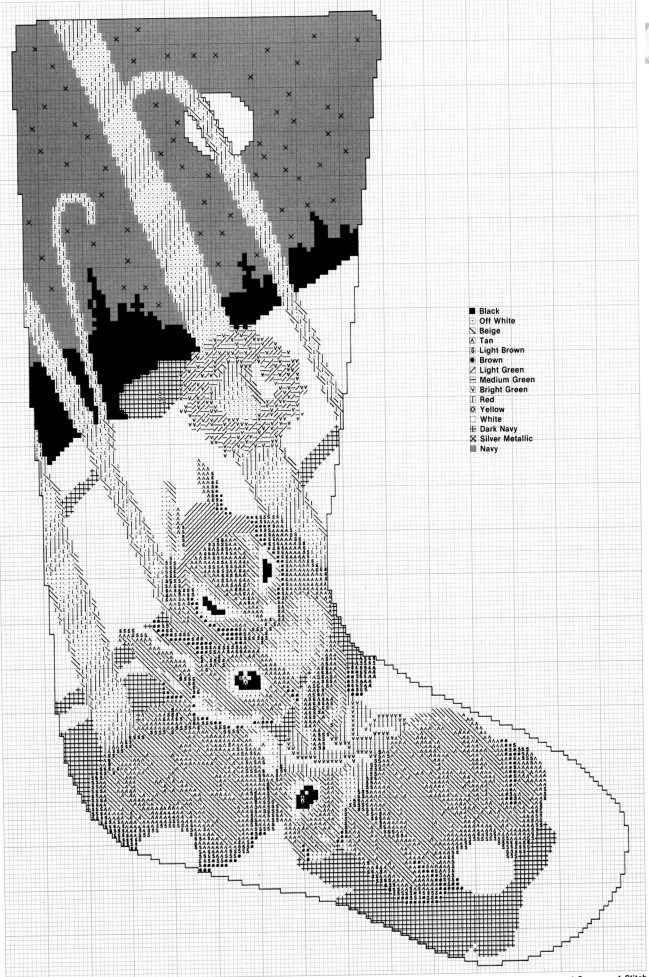

■ Black
⊡ Off White
◪ Beige
⋀ Tan
⒮ Light Brown
● Brown
⊿ Light Green
⊟ Medium Green
⋁ Bright Green
⊞ Red
◎ Yellow
☐ White
⊞ Dark Navy
✕ Silver Metallic
▨ Navy

1 Square = 1 Stitch

Storybook Stocking to Needlepoint

• Unless otherwise noted, use basic tent stitches (either use basket-weave stitches for large areas of color or continental stitches for outlining and small areas of color) throughout the design. See diagrams, *right.*

• To begin stitching, tie a waste knot as follows: Thread the needle, knot the end of the yarn, and insert the needle into the canvas from front to back so the knot is on the front of your work. Stitch over the thread end to secure it; clip the knot and pull the yarn end to the back of the work.

• Maintain even tension as you stitch so that the yarn completely covers the canvas and the stitches look uniform.

• To end a strand of yarn, secure the end by carefully weaving it through the backs of stitches already worked.

To begin stitching, first work the black border of trees and shadows in the distant background; fill in the entire area with black yarn. Then begin working the candy canes in the colors indicated on the pattern.

Stitch the moon as indicated and fill in the remaining sky with navy yarn. For each star, work one cross-stitch in silver thread on top of the navy sky as indicated on the pattern.

Work the wreath and add red French knots on it at random.

Work the three rabbits in various shades of brown, off-white, and white. Stitch the eyes in black.

Next, work the rabbits' hats according to the pattern. On the tallest rabbit's hat, alternate the direction of the stitches to simulate knitting, if desired.

To make two cotton tails, use white yarn and work in turkey loop stitches (see the diagram). Clip the loops and brush the yarn gently.

Fill in the remaining shadow areas using dark navy yarn. Work the remaining areas of snow using white yarn.

When all of the needlepoint is complete, remove the canvas from the frame; block it following the instructions on page 32.

• To finish the stocking, cut out the stitched needlepoint design, leaving ½ inch of unworked canvas all around. From navy velvet, cut a backing that is the same size as the front.

With right sides facing, stitch together the stocking front and back using a ½-inch seam allowance (sew between the first and second rows of stitching on the needlepoint). Leave top open. Clip curves; trim seams.

• To line the stocking, trace the shape of the stocking onto lining fabric. Add a ½-inch seam allowance, then cut a front and back. With the right sides together, stitch, leaving the top edge open.

With wrong sides together, slip the lining over the stocking. Stitch together along the top, using a ½-inch seam allowance. Turn the stocking right side out; tuck lining inside.

Whipstitch purchased cording to the side and top edges of the stocking. Add a hanging loop at the top.

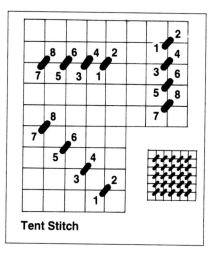

Tent Stitch

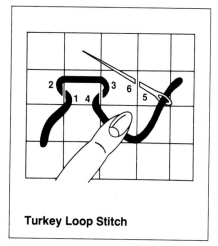

Turkey Loop Stitch

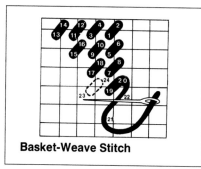

Basket-Weave Stitch

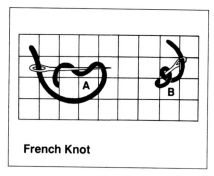

French Knot

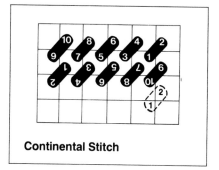

Continental Stitch

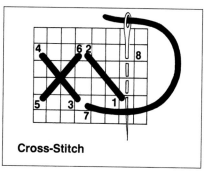

Cross-Stitch

In every stitch, this charming pair of embroideries captures the childlike excitement of Christmas around the family tree.

MATERIALS

(For both pictures)
½ yard of white linen
½ yard of polka dot fabric
⅛ yard of blue tulle
Embroidery floss in the colors
   listed on page 63
Two silver stars
Two sets of 12- and 14-inch
   artist's stretcher strips
Staple gun, sawtooth hangers
Dressmaker's carbon paper

INSTRUCTIONS

Trace the full-size patterns on pages 62-63 onto paper. Center each of the designs on 14x16 inches of linen; transfer to the fabric with dressmaker's carbon paper.

Assemble stretcher strips according to the manufacturer's instructions. Staple the right side of the fabric to the *back* of each of the assembled frames.

For each design, cut three layers of tulle to fit the window area; baste to linen.

Embroider the pictures according to the diagrams and color key. Or, experiment with different colors (see pages 62-63). Use two strands of floss for the faces, six strands for the rest of the design. Braid floss for girl's pigtail. Attach stars to the treetops with French knots.

To frame *each* of the stitcheries, cut two 16x20-inch rectangles from polka dot fabric. Sew a 7½-inch-diameter circle in center of each. Cut out each circle ¼ inch inside stitching. Clip curves; turn under raw edges.

Place the rectangles wrong sides together, matching the cutout circles. Blindstitch the rectangles together around the circle. Stretch fabric across top of frame; staple to the back.

If desired, embellish frames with bows; add sawtooth hangers to the backs.

Continued

STITCHES

A. French knot
B. Chain stitch
C. Satin stitch
D. Straight stitch
E. Split stitch
F. Long & short stitch

The appeal of these embroideries is due largely to their vivid colors. Because the designs call for a small amount of floss in each color, you may wish to use leftovers you have on hand. We've listed the basic colors you need, leaving it up to you to choose the shades within those color ranges.

If you want to use up scraps of floss in colors that aren't included in the key, you can experiment with changing the color of some of the components in the design. For instance, while you

may not wish to alter Santa's bright red suit or the green Christmas tree, the children's hair and clothing can be whatever colors you wish.

Before you begin stitching, though, it's important to judge the overall impact of the colors you've chosen. A good test of color compatibility is to lay all the floss side by side, then stand back from it and squint. If the color "blur" appeals to you, you will probably be happy with your choices when the pictures are embroidered.

COLORS

1. Dk. green	7. Orange
2. Med. green	8. Yellow
3. Lt. green	9. Flesh
4. Red	10. White
5. Brown	11. Gray
6. Tan	12. Black

CHRISTMAS QUILTS & COMFORTS

Surround your loved ones with the warmth of the holidays by making a quilt or afghan with the spirit of the season stitched right in.

On the following pages, you'll find comforters, such as this appliquéd poinsettia quilt, designed especially for Christmas. Others are stitched for stylish snuggling all winter long. But whether they are quilted, knitted, or crocheted, all the hand-stitched comforts in this chapter will spread joy to your family and friends.

With its fanciful arrangement of appliquéd flowers and quilted star and circle motifs, the antique poinsettia quilt on pages 64-65 is a treasured reflection of the holiday spirit. Stitch this lovely heritage quilt to share with houseguests and family members for years to come.

The completed quilt measures 82x91 inches.

MATERIALS

10 yards of unbleached muslin (5 yards for quilt top; 5 yards for backing)
2 yards of red cotton
Scraps of green and yellow cotton
82x91 inches of quilt batting
Blue pearl cotton embroidery thread
Off-white quilting thread
Graph paper
Sandpaper or cardboard for templates
Quilting frame or hoop
Red seam binding or bias tape

INSTRUCTIONS

The quilt has a total of nine poinsettia designs—one in each corner, one centered along each side, and one in the middle. Each poinsettia is different, but all are adapted from the same basic pattern, *right.*

If you want to make a quilt like ours, refer to the photograph for the adaptations of the poinsettia pattern. But if you wish, you can alter the pattern, adjusting the size and shape of the poinsettias to fit your quilt.

For instance, you can appliqué two poinsettias in one flowerpot, or show them without the flowerpot. Whatever you decide, sketch the quilt you intend to make to be sure you're satisfied with the overall design.

Before cutting the appliqués, preshrink all the fabric. Enlarge the pattern, *below right.* Number the individual shapes in the appliqué design and note how many of each shape you'll need to cut.

To make the templates, trace each pattern piece onto sandpaper or cardboard. Do not add seam allowances. Because the flower petals are not all the same shape, make a template for each. When you have traced all the pieces, carefully cut out the templates.

With a hard lead pencil, lightly draw around each template on the fabric, leaving at least ½ inch between the pieces to allow for ¼-inch seam allowances all around. Trace around the templates for all appliqué pieces before you begin to cut.

When cutting out the fabric shapes, cut ¼ inch beyond the pencil lines. After cutting the appliqués, sort them according to shape and color. Turn under seam allowances on the appliqués, then baste and press.

Cut and piece the muslin top to 72x81 inches. Lay muslin out flat and arrange the appliqués in place. When you are pleased with the arrangement, pin and baste appliqués to the muslin; whipstitch them into place.

Where the stem, flowerpot, and petals overlap more than ¼ inch, trim excess fabric from the bottom shape to reduce bulk and eliminate shadows.

When you have appliquéd all the pieces, make a border for the quilt: Cut and piece 5½-inch-wide strips of red fabric to equal the length of the quilt sides. Then, using a ¼-inch seam allowance, stitch the two strips to each side of the quilt

top. Following the same procedure, cut, piece, and stitch borders for the ends of the quilt.

To prepare for quilting, cut and piece a muslin backing to match the quilt top. Layer the backing, batting, and quilt top. If you don't plan to use a full-size frame for quilting, baste the layers together from the center toward the sides and corners, and around the edges.

Stretch the quilt in a frame or hoop. Quilt around each appliqué, then stitch the background in the pattern of your choice. We used blue pearl cotton to work five-pointed stars (each approximately 10 inches in diameter), and 4-inch-diameter circles stitched at random between stars and appliqués.

For a star pattern, make a template of a star from cardboard or sandpaper. Using a pencil, lightly trace around the template wherever you want the stars to appear on the quilt. Quilt over the outlines using small running stitches.

Finish the outside edges of the quilt with red seam binding or bias tape.

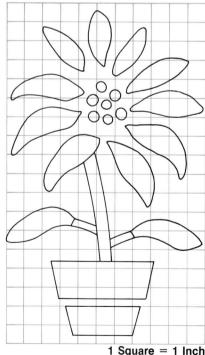

1 Square = 1 Inch

Carefully preserved in the Kentucky home of George Rogers Clark, one of America's great explorers, this beautiful grapevine and flowers coverlet is a masterpiece of the quiltmaker's art. The traditional red and green fabrics used in the design make it a special joy to stitch and quilt for the holiday season.

MATERIALS

4½ yards of 45-inch-wide muslin or off-white broadcloth
3 yards of 45-inch-wide green fabric
1½ yards each of cranberry red and brown fabric
¼ yard of a red and white print fabric
⅛ yard of yellow fabric
Red, green, and brown thread
White quilting thread
72-inch-square quilt batting
Green embroidery floss
5½ yards of green piping
4¼ yards of 45-inch-wide off-white backing fabric
19x24 inches of tissue paper
Cardboard for templates

INSTRUCTIONS

Before you begin, study the layout of this 72-inch-square quilt. The center of the quilt is made by joining four 24-inch appliquéd blocks into a square. The resulting 48-inch square is bordered by eight blocks, each 12x24 inches. A 12-inch square
Continued

67

is then stitched in each corner. See assembly directions, *below.*

For quilt block layouts and appliqué templates, enlarge patterns A and B, *below right,* onto tissue paper as follows:

In each 24-inch block in the middle of the quilt, the flower is in the center. To make this symmetrical design, trace pattern A four times, flopping the pattern along fold lines.

For the border block, trace pattern B twice, flopping the design at the center. For the corner block, trace over pattern A, omitting the two half leaves along fold lines and ignoring the fold lines.

To make templates for appliqués, trace onto cardboard one grape leaf with stem, one grape, three parts of the vine (the stem and branches), and each layer of the flower. Cut out pieces.

To make appliqués, use a pencil to draw around cardboard templates onto fabrics. Leave ½-inch spaces between pencil lines to allow for a ¼-inch seam allowance around each piece.

Draw the following: on green fabric, 112 grape leaves, 112 stems, 540 grapes, and 14 outer flower shapes; on the cranberry red, 1,080 grapes and 14 each of the two red flower shapes (see pattern B); on brown, 36 of each of the 3 vine pieces. Also draw 14 red-and-white print flower shapes and 14 yellow centers.

Cut around pieces *¼ inch from pencil lines;* set aside.

From the off-white fabric, cut out four 25-inch squares, eight 13x25-inch rectangles, and four 13-inch squares. Appliqué each piece of the grape and flower designs onto blocks, using the layout drawings as guides for placement of the pieces.

Pin appliqué pieces to muslin blocks; turn raw edges under, clipping where needed. Fold the pencil lines under just enough to hide them; whipstitch shapes

in place. With three strands of floss, use stem stitches to embroider tendrils on the bunches of grapes.

• *For a quicker and less expensive quilt,* substitute acrylic fabric paints for appliqué fabrics, using the diagrams, *below right,* as painting guides.

First, enlarge the patterns. Slip the drawings underneath the muslin and position them in place. (The design will be visible through the fabric.) Dip a fine-tip brush into paint (stroke off excess paint on paper toweling), and brush the color sparingly onto fabric. Paint *up to but not over* design lines.

To complete the design, flop the quilt patterns as instructed above for the appliquéd quilt and paint all components of the design using the same colors as you would use for appliqués. When all blocks are painted and dry, heat-set colors with a warm iron on the *wrong* side of the fabric.

• **Assembling the quilt:** Using ½-inch seam allowances, construct the quilt top as follows: Join the four 24-inch blocks into a 48-inch square. Then, with raw edges together, sew green piping around the perimeter of the large square.

To make each end border of the quilt, sew two rectangular blocks together end to end; join them to opposite ends of large square. (See the photograph.)

Make two border strips for the sides. For each strip, join two rectangular blocks end to end; join corner blocks at each end of the strip. Join strips to the sides of the quilt. Press seams open; press the quilt top on the wrong side.

To make a backing for the quilt, cut the backing fabric in half crosswise. Open out the pieces and join them along the selvage edges with a ½-inch seam allowance. Press the seam open. Then layer the quilt top, batting, and backing.

If you plan to quilt with a hoop, baste the quilt layers together. Lay the backing on the floor, wrong side up. Lay the batting on the backing, then the quilt top on the batting. Pin the layers together with long florist's pins.

With long running stitches, baste the layers together horizontally and vertically through the quilt center. Baste two diagonal lines from corner to corner; baste around outside edges.

Stretch the quilt in a frame or hoop and, with tiny running stitches, quilt around all the design elements and along the leaf veins. Across plain muslin, quilt diagonal rows 1 inch apart, as shown in the photograph. (For more details about quilting, see pages 70-71.)

When quilting is completed, bind edges with green bias tape.

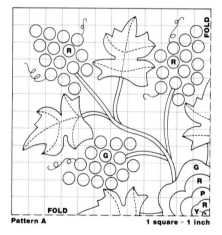

Pattern A   1 square = 1 inch

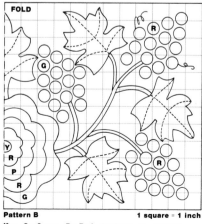

Pattern B   1 square = 1 inch
Key G = Green R = Red P = Pink Y = Yellow

Appliquéd squares of Christmas motifs are set together with bright sashing strips to create a comforter that's not only warm and cozy, but also fashioned in the spirit of the season.

The appliqués are stylized versions of traditional Christmas symbols, all surrounded with garland borders and highlighted with bits of embroidery.

A holly leaf quilting pattern completes the festive stitching on this 75-inch-square quilt.

MATERIALS
6½ yards of white fabric
2 yards of red fabric
9 yards of wide red bias tape
75x75 inches of quilt batting
Scraps of fabrics in assorted
  colors for appliqués
Embroidery floss, hoop, needle
Water erasable craft marker
Thread in colors to match
  appliqué fabrics

INSTRUCTIONS
To make the quilt, you will need to appliqué motifs to nine white squares, then join the squares with red and white sashing strips. To begin, cut all the quilt blocks and sashing strips. From white fabric, cut nine 18¾-inch-square blocks and 24 strips, each 3¼x23½ inches. From the red fabric, cut 48 strips, each 1¾x23½ inches.

Using a ⅜-inch seam allowance, sew a red strip to each long side of a white strip, making 24 sashing strips. Recut the ends of the sashing strips in a V as indicated on the pattern on page 70.

From the remaining red fabric, cut 32 strips 1¾ inches wide and about 5 inches long. These will be appliquéd in the corners between blocks. Turn under ⅜ inch on the long raw edges; press. Set aside.

Continued

69

Album Quilt

With a dark marking pen, enlarge the pattern for each of the squares, *opposite*. These will be your master patterns.

From cardboard or fine sandpaper, cut a template for each of the major elements in the motifs. (Design details will be embroidered later.) Note that the same border motifs are used on blocks directly or diagonally opposite each other on the quilt.

On fabric in colors of your choice, trace around the templates, leaving ½ inch between the tracings. Cut out the pieces, adding a ¼-inch seam allowance all around.

To appliqué the pieces to the squares, turn under the seam allowance on each piece; baste and press. Following the master patterns, position the appliqués on white squares so that the designs are centered. Pin all the pieces in place; whipstitch.

When you have appliquéd all the pieces, add touches of embroidery for the narrow lines, centers of flowers, and other design details.

To join the nine appliquéd blocks, stitch them together with sashing strips in between, leaving the last ⅜ inch of the seams unsewn at each end. Sew the points of the strips together as shown, *below left.*

To make the red X between each block, measure diagonally between blocks, corner to corner. Trim the 5-inch-long red strips to this measurement, adding ⅜-inch seam allowances *on each end.*

Turn under the seam allowances on the ends and press. Then position the strips in an X atop the diagonal seams in the sashing strips. Blindstitch the strips to the sashing.

To fill in triangular spaces along the outer edges of the top, cut white triangles, using the sashing strip pattern as a guide (add ⅜-inch seam allowances). Sew the triangles between red strips in the corners and along the sides of the quilt.

Enlarge the holly leaf quilting pattern, *left,* and make a template of the pattern. With a water-erasable craft marker or hard lead pencil, trace around the template on the sashing strips from X to X.

Also, mark a 1-inch grid quilting pattern within the blocks.

Mark the grid lines up to, but not over, the appliqués.

To assemble the quilt, cut and piece white fabric until it is the same size as the quilt top. Sandwich the batting between the top and backing.

• **Basting the quilt:** If you intend to quilt without a quilting frame, lay the backing facedown on the floor and smooth it out so the grain is straight and the corners are square. Place the batting on top of the backing. Then place the pressed and marked quilt top over the batting. Smooth it out and square the corners.

Use long florist's pins spaced about 8 inches apart to pin through all three layers, starting in the center and going in all directions. Be sure to smooth out any lumps and wrinkles as you go along.

With a 1-inch running stitch, baste the three layers together along the lengthwise and crosswise grains through the center of the quilt, then diagonally from corner to corner and around the outside edges.

• **Quilting by hand:** Mount the quilt in a floor frame, or stretch it in a quilting hoop. Use waxed quilting thread and a No. 8 or 9 sharp needle. Work with a single 20-inch-long quilting thread.

Knot the end of the thread and, working from the bottom, bring the needle up through all three layers. Pull the knot through the backing until it's concealed in the batting.

To stitch, follow one of two methods. One method is to keep your right hand above the quilt and your left hand below it. Push the needle down through all thicknesses with the right hand, then push it up with the left hand close to the first stitch. The stitches should be the same length on both sides.

If you are left-handed, keep the left hand atop the quilt and the right hand beneath it.

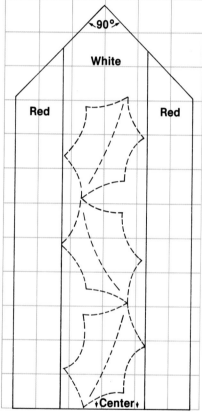

1 Square = 1 Inch

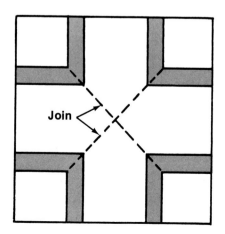

The other method is to take two or three running stitches at a time before pulling the thread through. Work the needle back and forth to catch all three layers on the needle, and keep your left hand under the quilt to feel for the needle and make sure it penetrates the layers.

Stitch over all the quilting lines marked on the quilt top.

When you have finished, remove the quilt from the frame or hoop and carefully take out any basting stitches.

• **Binding the quilt:** If you are using purchased bias tape, you may have to stitch together several lengths of tape to extend all around the quilt. To do so, put the short ends of two strips together, right sides facing, and

stitch with the grain in a ¼-inch seam. Press the seam flat.

With right sides together, pin bias tape to the quilt top, starting in the middle of a side. Sew around all the edges of the quilt to secure the tape, keeping the corners neat and square. Trim away the excess fabric and fold the tape to the back. Pin the tape in place; blindstitch.

1 Space = 2 Inches

Like old-time quilts that inspired it, this crocheted afghan combines hand-spun warmth with a classic country spirit.

The granny squares that comprise this festive afghan require just two colors of yarn, and are crocheted one at a time. (Take one along on a holiday errand to fill in any spare moments).

When set together in the ever-popular Ohio Star pattern, the red and white blocks create a striking contrast of stars and squares, with a mock sawtooth border that's also a quilting tradition.

The result is an afghan fashioned for Christmas, but cozy enough for all winter long.

MATERIALS
4-ply knitting worsted
   yarn—64 ounces of red,
   36 ounces of ecru
Size H crochet hook
Yarn needle

INSTRUCTIONS
Make 109 red squares, 36 ecru squares, and 76 two-color squares, according to the following instructions.

Gauge: 1 square = 4 inches.

• **Solid-color square:** *Rnd 1:* Ch 3, join with sl st to form ring. Ch 4 (counts as 1 dc and ch 1) * 3 dc in ring, ch 1; rep from * twice more; 2 dc in ring and join with sl st by wrapping around ch 4, sl st in 4th ch.

Rnd 2: Do not turn. Ch 4, 3 dc in same corner sp, * 3 dc, ch 1, 3 dc in next corner, rep from * twice more; 2 dc in next corner, join with sl st by wrapping around ch 4, sl st in 4th ch.

Rnds 3-4: Rep Rnd 2 inc 1 grp of 3 dc bet corners each rnd. After joining on Rnd 4, fasten off.

• **Two-color square:** *Rnd 1:* With red, ch 3, join with sl st to form ring, ch 2, wrap hook with ecru (leave 3-inch tail) and ch 2 with ecru (counts as 1 dc and ch 1) 2 dc into ring with ecru (hold dropped color at back of work and crochet around it to carry it along hereafter) 1 dc in ring pulling red through 2nd 2 lps to pick up red and drop ecru; ch 1, 3 dc in ring with red, pulling ecru through last 2 lps of 3rd dc (drops red and picks up ecru; use this method of changing colors from now on except at beg corner); ch 1, 3 dc in ring changing color on 3rd dc; ch 1, 2 dc in ring, wrap around ch 4 and join with sl st, sl st into 4th ch.

Rnd 2: Do not turn. Ch 2 with red, wrap with ecru, ch 2, * 3 dc in same corner (wrapping around dropped color at back of work) 3 dc in next corner changing colors on 3rd dc, ch 1. Rep from * twice more. 3 dc in same corner, 2 dc in next corner, wrap around ch 4 and sl st to join, sl st into 4th ch.

Rnds 3-4: Rep Rnd 2 inc 1 grp of 3 dc bet corners each rnd. After joining 4th rnd, fasten off.

To assemble squares into the afghan, follow diagram, *right.*

The squares are crocheted together on the wrong side with single crochet and red yarn. Crochet all rows tog horizontally, then vertically.

Beg in lower right corner, match 1st square of Row 1 and 1st square of Row 2, right sides together. Insert hook through corner ch of each square, pull yarn through and sc. Insert hook through top 2 loops of next dc of each square and sc. Do not work too tightly or work will not lie flat. Continue this way across the row, matching corners as you go. Fasten off.

To finish afghan, attach yarn in any corner, ch 4 (1 dc and ch 1), 3 dc in same corner, dc in top 2 lps of each dc and corner ch across (14 dc for each square except for corner squares; 13 dc for corner squares). At end of row 3 dc, ch 1, 3 dc for corner. Continue around.

To finish last corner 2 dc, join with sl st by wrapping around ch 4. Fasten off.

Tuck in all ends with yarn needle by pushing the needle through threads (not between them) 1 inch in one direction and 1 inch in opposite direction. This gives ends a secure anchoring that does not easily pull apart and stands up well to machine washing and drying.

- **Blocking the afghan:** First, dampen the afghan and lay it flat on a sheet or several towels. With rustproof pins, secure the edges of the afghan to the sheet, then weight the corners to keep them from curling.

Cover the afghan with a damp, lint-free cloth. With an iron set at a moderate temperature, gently press the afghan. Apply light, even pressure, never holding the iron too long in one place. When you've pressed the entire afghan, let it dry completely; remove the pins.

- **Washing the afghan:** Look on the yarn label for instructions that specify whether the afghan should be cleaned professionally or can be laundered at home. If there are no instructions, hand-wash the afghan,

maintaining a warm temperature. Use a detergent especially made for knits or a mild soap.

Let the afghan soak for several minutes, then wash it by squeezing gently. (Never wring the afghan.) To help prevent distortion during the washing, support the afghan with your hands as much as possible.

Rinse the afghan thoroughly and gently squeeze out the excess water. Then block and dry, following the blocking instructions, *left.*

- **Storing the afghan:** If you plan to store the afghan for long periods of time, do not fold it; folds can damage the yarn. Instead, roll up the afghan and cover loosely with cotton fabric that will allow the afghan to "breathe."

Crochet Abbreviations

beg	begin(ning)
ch	chain
cl	cluster
dc	double crochet
dec	decrease, decreasing
dtr	double treble
grp	group
hdc	half double crochet
inc	increase, increasing
lp(s)	loop(s)
pat	pattern
rep	repeat
rnd	round
sc	single crochet
sl st	slip-stitch
sp(s)	space(s)
st(s)	stitch(es)
tr	treble crochet
tog	together
yo	yarn over
*	repeat from * as indicated

Christmas Patchwork to Knit

With its jolly colors and Christmas motifs, this knitted patchwork afghan is just Santa's style —spectacular enough to present to anyone on his Christmas list, and warm enough to keep him snug on long arctic nights.

MATERIALS

Bernat's Berella 4 (4-ply knitting worsted) or a suitable substitute in 4-ounce skeins in the following amounts and colors: 3 white (A); 2 scarlet (B); 1 each of tapestry green (C), honey (D), pale olive (E), walnut (F), baby blue (G), old gold (H), pumpkin (I), baby yellow (J), marine blue (K), willow (L), medium orange (M), caramel (N), and black (O)
Size 7 knitting needles, or size to obtain gauge given below
Size H aluminum crochet hook
Yarn needle
Gauge: 5 sts = 1 inch; 6 rows = 1 inch.
See knitting abbreviations on page 77.

INSTRUCTIONS

The afghan is made up of 55 rectangles, either plain or featuring a knitted-in pattern. The rectangles are joined to form eight blocks (indicated by the solid lines on the placement diagram on page 76). The blocks are joined to form the afghan, which is edged with a crocheted border. All knitting is stockinette stitch (k 1 row, p 1 row).

Refer to the diagram for colors and sizes of squares. When finishing each square, always bind off as if to knit.

• **How to read the placement diagram:** Each rectangle is represented on the diagram on page 76. A capital letter on a rectangle means that it is plain, without a knitted-in pattern. Knit that rectangle in the color corresponding to the capital letter in the materials list, *left.*

If the rectangle has a number followed by a lower case letter, the number refers to one of the patterns, and the letter refers to the color combination stated in the special instructions below. The background color for each rectangle is also specified in the special instructions.

The other numbers found on the diagram represent the size of each rectangle. For example, rectangle 6b centered along the top edge reads "60x50." The first number always refers to the amount of sts cast on, and the second refers to the amount of rows worked. This means that you cast on 60 sts, and work evenly for 50 rows.

• **Two-color knitting:** When working with two colors of yarn in a row, always twist the new yarn around the strand just worked to prevent any holes. Carry the unused color (or colors) loosely behind the work. If the unused color(s) is carried along for more than 5 or 6 sts, bring the color used under the unused color every 5 or 6 sts to prevent loose strands from floating across the back.

When a color is separated by a large number of sts for more than a row or two, use separate strands of that color.

• **Special instructions:**
1: Background is in color A.
2: Background is in color E.
3: Background is in color G.
4: Background is in color G.
5: Background is in color A.
5a: Cast on 20 sts in F. Work 7 rows in st st. Begin chart 5, referring only to the holly leaf design marked in black Xs, as follows: P 5 in F; attach E and p 1; p in F to end of row. On next row k 13 in F; k 1 in E; k 6 in F. Continue following chart in this manner until the leaf is completed. Work 6 more stockinette

rows in F, ending with a p row. Cast off all sts on next row.
5b: Follow instructions for 5a, substituting color O for color F, and color A for color E.
6a: Use A for background and I for figures.
6b: Use J for background and K for figures.
7a: Background is in color G.
7b: Use E for background, color C for L, color I for B, color M for middle flower and centers of other two flowers, and I for center of middle flower.
8a: Background is in color N.
8b: Use J for background; replace B with F.
9a: Use E for the background. Work 10 rows in E. On next row k 16 in E; attach C and k 1; attach L and k 1; k 1 in C; k to end of row in E.

Follow the next 5 rows of the chart, using 1 strand each of colors E, C, and L. Be careful to bring the threads of colors C and L around last unused color. At end of row, cut off color C thread, but carry same strand of color L up center of tree.

On next row k 3 in E; attach first strand of C and k 14; k 1 in L; k 14 in C; attach second strand of E and k 3. *Do not cut off thread of C* at end of row.

On next row p 3 in E; attach a second strand of L and follow chart across row. *Do not cut off second strand of L* at end of row. On next row, k 3 in E; attach a second strand of C; follow chart across next 2 rows without cutting off second strand of C.

On next row, k 4 in color E; pick up second strand of color L from the back and follow the chart to the end of the row. On the next row, p 4 in color C; pick up first strand of color C from back of work and continue across row. Follow rest of chart, continuing to work with 2 strands each of colors E, C, and L until tree is done. Carry color C and color L up back of work as suggested.

Continued

9b: Follow instructions for 9a, substituting color A for color E, color L for color C, and color C for color L.

10a: Background is in color J.

10b: Use color N for color J, color E for color C, color C for color E, color A for color K. (Color B stays the same.)

11a: Work the background in color N.

11b: Use color J for color N, color O for F, color D for M. (Color A stays the same.)

12a: Background is in color A.

12b: Substitute color B for H.

13a: Background is in color L.

13b: Use color C for color L, and color J for color E.

14a: Use color D for the background. Cast on 25 sts in color D and work 8 rows in st st. Begin following chart 14 as follows: K 7 in color D; attach color G and k 1; k 9 in color D; attach *second strand* of G and k 1; k 7 in D.

Continue following chart, using 2 separate strands of G, until the 7 pattern rows have been repeated 5 times (43 completed rows). Using only D, work 7 more stockinette rows, ending with a p row. Cast off all sts on the next row.

14b: Follow instructions for 14a, substituting color M for color D, and color A for color G.

14c: Cast on 25 sts in color L and work 5 rows in st st. Begin following chart 14 as follows: P 7 in color L; attach color H and p 1; p 9 in L, attach *second strand* of H and p 1; p 7 in L.

Continue following the chart, using 2 separate strands of color H, until the 7 pattern rows have been repeated 3 times (26 completed rows). Using only color L, work 4 more stockinette rows, ending with a p row. Cast off all sts on next row.

14d: Follow instructions for 14c, substituting color B for color L and color C for color H.

15a: Use color I for background. Cast on 50 sts in color I and work 6 rows in st st. Begin following chart 15:

Row 1: K 5 in color I; work across section A 6 times; work across section B once; k 4 in I.

Row 2: P 4 in color I; work across section B once, attaching N where indicated; work across section A 6 times; p 5 in I.

Repeat instructions for Rows 1 and 2 to end of chart (13 more times), always working from right to left on k rows and from left to right on p rows. Work 6 more rows in st st, using only color I, ending with a p row. Cast off all sts on next row.

15b: Follow instructions for 15a, substituting color K for color I, and color G for color N.

16a: Use color H for background. Cast on 40 sts in color H and work 9 rows in st st. Begin following chart 16:

Row 1: P 4 in color H; p across the chart (from left to right) 4 times, attaching J and working in where indicated; p 4 in H.

Row 2: K 4 in color H; k across chart (from right to left) 4 times, working in color J as indicated; k 4 in color H.

Repeat Rows 1 and 2 to end of chart, ending with Row 1 (a p row). Work 8 more rows in st st, using only H. End with a p row. Cast off all sts on the next row.

16b: Follow instructions for 16a, substituting color B for color H, and color N for color J.

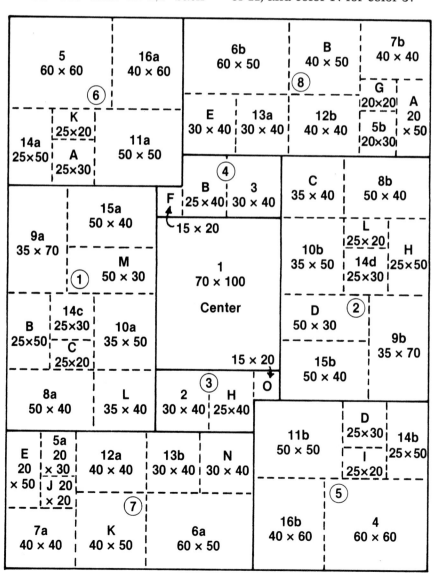

- **Sewing pieces together:** Tie off and weave in all yarn ends; block the pieces. With yarn and a tapestry needle, backstitch the pieces together from the reverse side, grouping the pieces as follows:

For best results when sewing pieces together, work so as to always end up with a rectangular finished piece. For example, in block 1, sew together 15a and color M piece, then sew both to 9a and put aside. Sew 14c to C piece, then sew both to color B piece and 10a and put aside. Sew 8a to L piece, then sew the 3 assembled pieces together.

Assemble blocks 1, 2, 3, and 4 separately. Sew blocks 3 and 4 to the bottom and top of center respectively. Sew block 1 to block 3, center, and block 4. Sew block 2 to block 3, center, and block 4.

Assemble blocks 5, 6, 7, and 8 separately. Sew blocks 5 and 7 together, lining up stitches as in diagram; then sew whole piece to blocks 1, 3, and 2. Sew blocks 6 and 8 together, again following diagram; then sew the whole piece to blocks 1, 4, and 2.

- **Crocheted border:** (See crocheting abbreviations on page 73.) With C, and a Size H aluminum crochet hook, work 2 rnds of sc all around, making 3 sc in each corner so that work lies flat. Change to A and work 1 rnd of sc; break off.

Next rnd: Working with B and H, work 3 sc of each color alternately around. (Carry unused color under the 3 sc group of the other color.) Continue around to starting point.

Next rnd: Repeat the previous rnd, working the same color sc above the previous row.

Next 3 rnds: Work 1 rnd in C and two rnds in B.

Picot edging: Attach color A, * make 1 sc in each of next 2 sts, ch 3, sl st to last sc just made, rep from * around. Fasten off.

Knitting Abbreviations

k.................knit
p.................purl
st(s).............stitch(es)
st st.............stockinette stitch
Continued

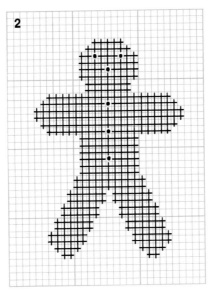

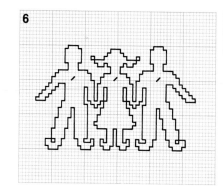

4

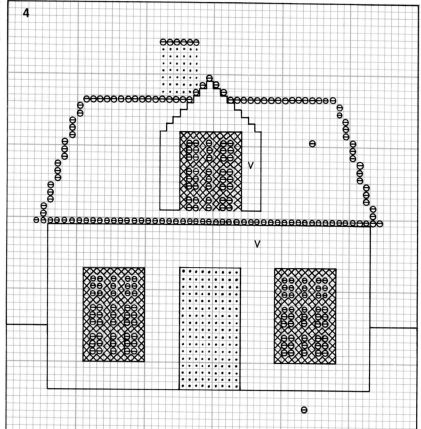

6

7

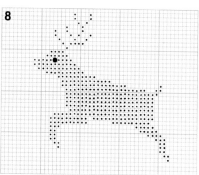

5

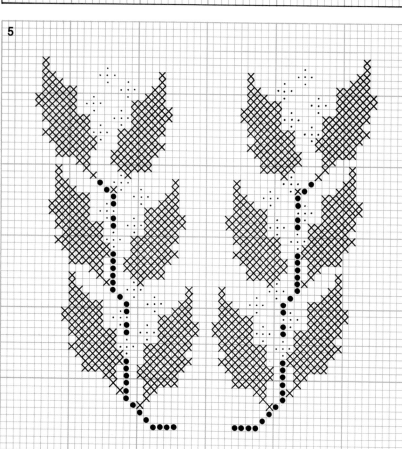

8

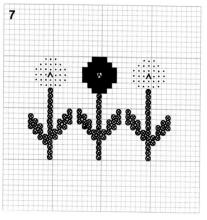

COLOR KEY

☐ Background
⊖ White
⊡ Scarlet
⊠ Tapestry Green
Ⅴ Honey
⊟ Pale Olive
⊞ Walnut
◺ Baby Blue
◹ Old Gold
◿ Pumpkin
○ Baby Yellow
■ Marine Blue
⊗ Willow
◫ Medium Orange
⊕ Caramel
⬢ Black

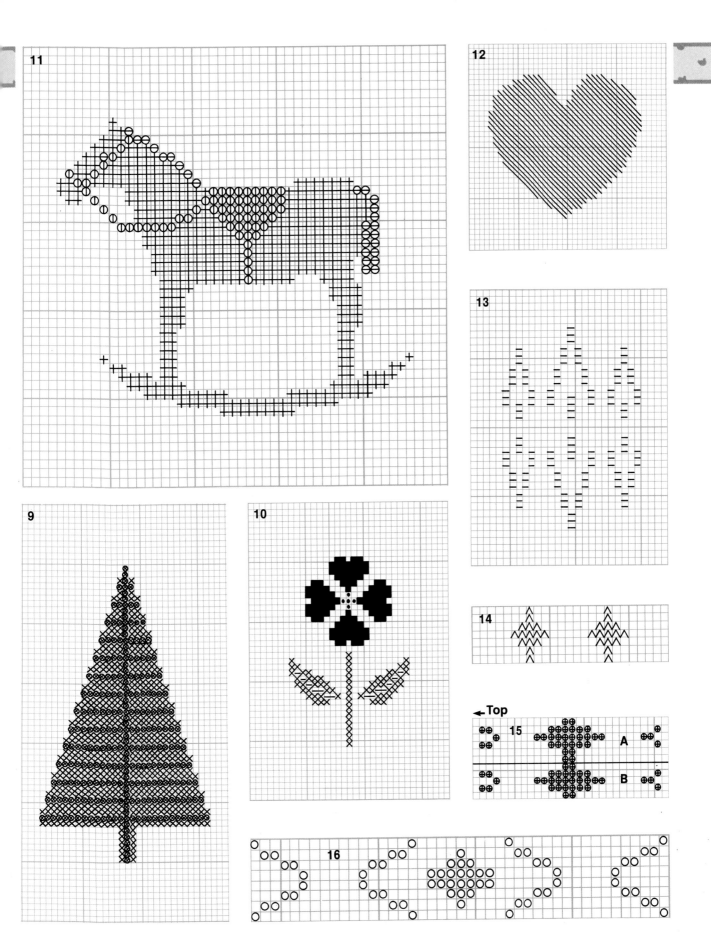

Acknowledgments

We extend our sincere thanks and appreciation to each of the following talented people who contributed craft designs and projects to this book.

Curt Boehringer—Twelve Days of Christmas Quilt, p. 26
Noreen Boyd—Floral Garland Ornaments, p. 4
Phyllis Dunstan—Della Robbia Wreath and Ornaments, p. 9; Cathedral Window "Pillows," p. 10
Hugie Dufresne—Sparkling Crocheted Lace, pp. 36-37
Elizabeth Ellsworth—Fantasy Father Christmas, p. 28
Pat Gardner—Christmas-Bright Ceramics, p. 45
Diane Marie Goff—Starry Crocheted Afghan, p. 73
Polly Gottfried—Christmas Tree Portraits, p. 61
Ruth Gray—Country Christmas Pillows, pp. 22-23
Kathy Sue Guillow—Album Quilt, p. 69
Sara Gutierrez—Whimsical Snowman to Stitch and Stuff, p. 56
Cynthia Hart—Victorian St. Nicholas, p. 35
Helen Hayes—Holiday Dance in Needlepoint, p. 31

Laura Holtorf—Cheery Cross-Stitch Towel, p. 25; Rose Place Mats, p. 41
Rebecca Jerdee—Playtime Village, pp. 48-49
Marcia Lentz—Snowflakes to Macrame, p. 13
Janet McCaffery—Elegant Beaded Angel, p. 18; Wreathful of Toys, p. 52; Yesteryear Stocking, p. 55
Virginia McCarthy—Christmas Patchwork to Knit, p. 74
Carrie Murphy—Snowflakes to Crochet, p. 13
Donald Nicholls—Sleigh Centerpiece, p. 46
Katie Ragsdale—Design on Sleigh Centerpiece, p. 46
Ruth Thogerson—Cross-Stitch Medallions, p. 17
Sara Jane Treinen—Sparkling Crocheted Bell Edging, pp. 36-37
James Williams—Needlepoint Storybook Stocking, p. 58
Judy Williamson—Floral Garland Tree Skirt and Stocking, pp. 4-5

We are also happy to acknowledge the following photographers, whose creative talents and technical skills contributed much to this book.

Ross Chapple—p. 67
Mike Dieter—Cover, pp. 10, 13, 46, 52
Jim Hedrich, for Hedrich-Blessing—pp. 55, 56

William Hopkins, for Hopkins Associates—pp. 4-5, 18, 22-23, 25, 26, 28, 31, 35, 36-37, 41, 42, 45, 48-49, 58, 61, 64-65, 69, 73, 74
Bradley Olman—pp. 9, 17

For their cooperation and courtesy, we extend a special thanks to:

David Friedlander Antiques, Louisville, Kentucky, Festive Poinsettia Quilt, pp. 64-65
Living History Farms, Des Moines, Iowa

Locust Grove, Louisville, Kentucky, for the use of the Keepsake Coverlet, p. 67
Pella Historical Society, Pella, Iowa